# Excel
*for*
WINDOWS 95
## FOR BUSY PEOPLE

D1309709

# Excel *for*

WINDOWS 95

## FOR BUSY PEOPLE

Osborne/**McGraw-Hill**
2600 Tenth Street
Berkeley, California 94710
U.S.A.

For information on translations or book distributors outside the U.S.A., or to arrange bulk purchase discounts for sales promotions, premiums, or fundraisers, please contact Osborne/**McGraw-Hill** at the above address.

**Excel for Windows 95 for Busy People**

1234567890 DOC 99876

ISBN 0-07-882111-8


Publisher:  Lawrence Levitsky
Acquisitions Editor:  Joanne Cuthbertson
Project Editor:  Claire Splan
Proofreader: Stefany Otis
Graphic Artist:  Marla J. Shelasky
Computer Designers:  Leslee Bassin, Roberta Steele
Quality Control: Joe Scuderi
Series and Cover Design: Ted Mader Associates
Series Illustration: Daniel Barbeau

**To my two fine sons—**
**You should both be very proud of yourselves.**
**Love, Dad**

**About the Author**

Ron Mansfield is a microcomputer consultant and author of *Windows 95 for Busy People* (Osborne/McGraw-Hill) and *The Compact Guide to Microsoft Office Professional* (Sybex). He has also written best-selling books on Microsoft Word for Windows and DOS 6.2. Mansfield is a frequent lecturer at national computer seminars and has written hundreds of articles for industry magazines and newsletters.

# Contents
## at a glance

**CHAPTERS**

# Contents

# ACKNOWLEDGMENTS

**This all started with Joanne Cuthbertson. Talk about a Renaissance Woman! Besides introducing me to Osborne, and to publisher Larry Levitsky, Joanne played a key role in developing not only this book, but the entire *Busy People* series. And she whipped my agent into line, and she picked me up at the airport, and she cheered me when I was down, and she made me make a schedule. Thanks, JC.**

When I first met fellow busy person Larry Levitsky (whose idea it was to create the *Busy People* series), I told him I wanted to work with a team of talented people doing something ground-breaking. He promised that I could, and he was right. Thanks again for inviting me to join Osborne/McGraw-Hill, and for letting me share in your vision, Larry!

Was it the design of this book that first attracted you? The promise of a great design was one of the reasons I joined the team. I am in awe of artists. They are like musicians—except they use pencils and markers (and now computers). The distinctive look and organization of this book was the result of the collaborative efforts of Ted Mader and Mary Jo Kovarik of Ted Mader Associates and Osborne's Marla Shelasky. The drawings and characters wandering through the pages were created by Dan Barbeau. Clever, yes?

My deadlines for this book collided with enough life complications to remind at least one of my friends of a soap opera. When it was clear that I was going to be unable to deliver Chapters 10 and 11 on time, Alan Neibauer jumped into the surf and pulled my butt out—this while he had his own share of stress and aggravation. Thanks, Alan. I owe ya one!

Authors grumble about editors, but we love 'em. And in truth, there wasn't even much to grumble about this trip. Both of my editors—project and copy editor Claire Splan and technical editor Heidi Steele—were gracious, thoughtful, and accommodating, despite impossible deadlines and much chaos. And the team wouldn't have been complete without the spirit of editorial assistant Heidi Poulin who helped keep all of us on track. It would be my pleasure to work with all of you again in the very near future.

Once written, and rewritten, and cut and expanded and cut some more, the manuscript was off to production, where ideas actually become books. Marla Shelasky headed up a talented team of typesetters, including Leslee Bassin, Roberta Steele, Lance Ravella, Peter H. Hancik, Richard Whitaker, and quality control specialist Joe Scuderi. I also owe special thanks to executive editor Scott Rogers, who contributed crucial energy and marketing acumen; controller Katharine Johnson, who backed us from the beginning; and Kendal Andersen, whose original marketing concepts were crucial to the successful launch of the series.

As always, my hat's off to the Osborne/McGraw-Hill sales folk who convince bookstores to make room on their crowded store shelves for my work; and to you bookstore buyers who keep saying "yes."

Finally, I want to thank *you readers* for purchasing this and my other books. Many of you have helped spread the word by telling your friends and family about my creations. It's truly appreciated.

Thanks again, each and every one of you! I have to run. My next manuscript for this series is going to be behind schedule if I don't ...

# INTRODUCTION

**When Osborne/McGraw-Hill approached me about their new *Busy People* series, I couldn't wait to get started! The publisher was looking for authors who understand that many readers have only a night or a few lunch hours to learn a new software package. Certainly the digital revolution has empowered us, but it has also accelerated everyone's expectations. How often do people say to you "fax me that budget," or "e-mail me those statistics," or "our product release has been moved up due to competitive pressures," or "it took longer than we thought—can you make up the time at your end?"**

To meet these needs, the editors expected opinionated, thoughtfully organized writing with a touch of skepticism. Fat-free fun. It was a perfect match. I hope you enjoy reading this book at least as much as I enjoyed writing it.

## I KNOW YOU'RE IN A HURRY, SO ...

Let's cut to the chase. If you haven't yet installed Excel for Windows 95, turn to Appendix A. If you are unfamiliar with Windows 95, you might want to read Appendix B next, since it will give you an overview. Or better yet, pick up a copy of my *Windows 95 for Busy People* book and start there.

Once you are up and running Excel, I suggest cruising Chapter 1 and reading Chapter 2 first, but you'll be fine no matter how much you bounce around. In a remarkably short period of time, you'll be able to:

- Start and quit Excel
- Create great looking workbooks and worksheets
- Get online help
- Use and create templates

- Rearrange and reformat worksheets
- Deal with printing and font issues
- Personalize the look, feel, and sound of Excel
- Organize large spreadsheet projects
- Use Excel's built-in functions for complex computations
- Display numbers in powerful, convincing graphs, and even create maps
- Harness macros to speed repetitive tasks
- Audit, troubleshoot, protect, and share your worksheets

Remember, though, just because you *can* do something with Excel doesn't mean that you *should*. Simple is often best, particularly when you are busy. I'll try to remind you of that from time to time.

# Excel for Windows 95: The Next Generation

If you've used earlier versions of Excel, you'll appreciate this next step in the evolutionary process. Excel is now Windows 95 savvy, which is to say it can use long filenames, sports new, easier-to-use Open and Save boxes, and much more.

You'll also enjoy the AutoCalculate feature which can give you answers without your needing to create formulas—simply select cells and let Excel calculate the sum of the cells, or their average, and so on. The AutoComplete feature watches you type and can guess what you might be planning to type next, saving you many keystrokes. The Data Map displays worksheet data on maps of the world, making it easy to show regional perspectives. There are new templates and an improved Template Wizard, as well.

Microsoft says it is moving toward a time where we will all think more about our *data* and less about specific, name brand *programs* used to create them. The lines are already blurring when we employ tools like object linking and embedding (OLE). If you believe the Microsoft public relations blitz, one day you'll forget about Microsoft Word and Excel and PowerPoint and just assemble menus of your favorite data-manipulating commands. Naturally, Microsoft will be selling us these tools, or perhaps building them into Windows 99. There are many miles to go before this becomes a reality, if ever. But in any case, I'll point out a few of the signposts for these new directions and try to get you into the habit of thinking about documents and tasks rather than just about programs.

Most of this is accomplished without sacrificing performance. In fact, many things (like printing) usually happen faster now, thanks to 32-bit support and other Windows 95 advancements.

# Things You Might Want to Know About This Book

You can read this book more or less in any order. Use the book as a reference, or read it cover to cover. Here's a quick rundown of the important elements you'll encounter as you go.

## Fast Forward

Each chapter begins with a section called *Fast Forward*. These sections should always be your first stop if you are a confident user, or impatient, or habitually late. You should find everything you need to get back on stride. Think of them as the *Reader's Digest* version of each chapter. This shorthand may leave you hungry, especially if you are new to Windows or Excel, so for more complete and leisurely explanations of techniques and shortcuts, read the rest of the chapter.

Fast Forwards are, in effect, a book within a book—a built-in quick reference guide summarizing the key tasks explained in each chapter. Written step by step, point by point, Fast Forwards also include illustrations and page references to guide you to the more complete information later in the chapter.

## Habits & Strategies

Don't overlook the *Habits* & *Strategies* notes. These short paragraphs suggest timesaving tips, techniques, and worthwhile addictions. (I've included them because, as Mark Twain once said, "Nothing so needs reforming as other people's habits.")

These habits and strategies also give you the big picture and help you plan ahead. For example, the long filenames you can use in Windows 95 and Excel are great, but they cause some interesting problems if you share files with users of Windows 3.1. So I've included some suggested file-naming strategies.

### Shortcuts

*Shortcuts* are designed with the busy person in mind. When there's a way to do something that may not be as fancy as the material in the text, but is *faster*, it will be described in the margin and highlighted by the special Shortcut icon.

### Cautions

Sometimes it's just too easy to plunge ahead, fall down a rabbit hole, and spend hours of extra time finding your way back to where you were before you went astray. This hard hat will warn you before you commit potentially time-consuming mistakes.

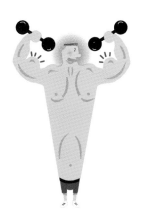

### Definitions

Usually, I'll explain computer jargon in the text when the techno-babble first occurs. But occasionally, you'll see this body builder icon in the margin. Most of the time these definitions are informal and often a little playful.

### Step-by-Step

*Step-by-Step* boxes will walk you through the necessary steps of everyday tasks, using annotated illustrations.

### Upgrade Notes

If you've used earlier versions of Excel, be on the look-out for *upgrade notes*. They will tell you when something has changed and make sure you don't miss any of the latest advances.

*Throughout the book, cross-references and other minor asides appear in margin notes like this one.*

## Let's Do It!

Ready? Hang out the Do Not Disturb sign, open that Jolt cola, and let's dig into Excel for Windows 95 before Excel for Windows 96 arrives!

Incidentally, I'm always happy to hear your reactions to this or any of my other books. You can reach me through the publisher or on the Net (**rmansfield@aol.com**).

# CHAPTER 1

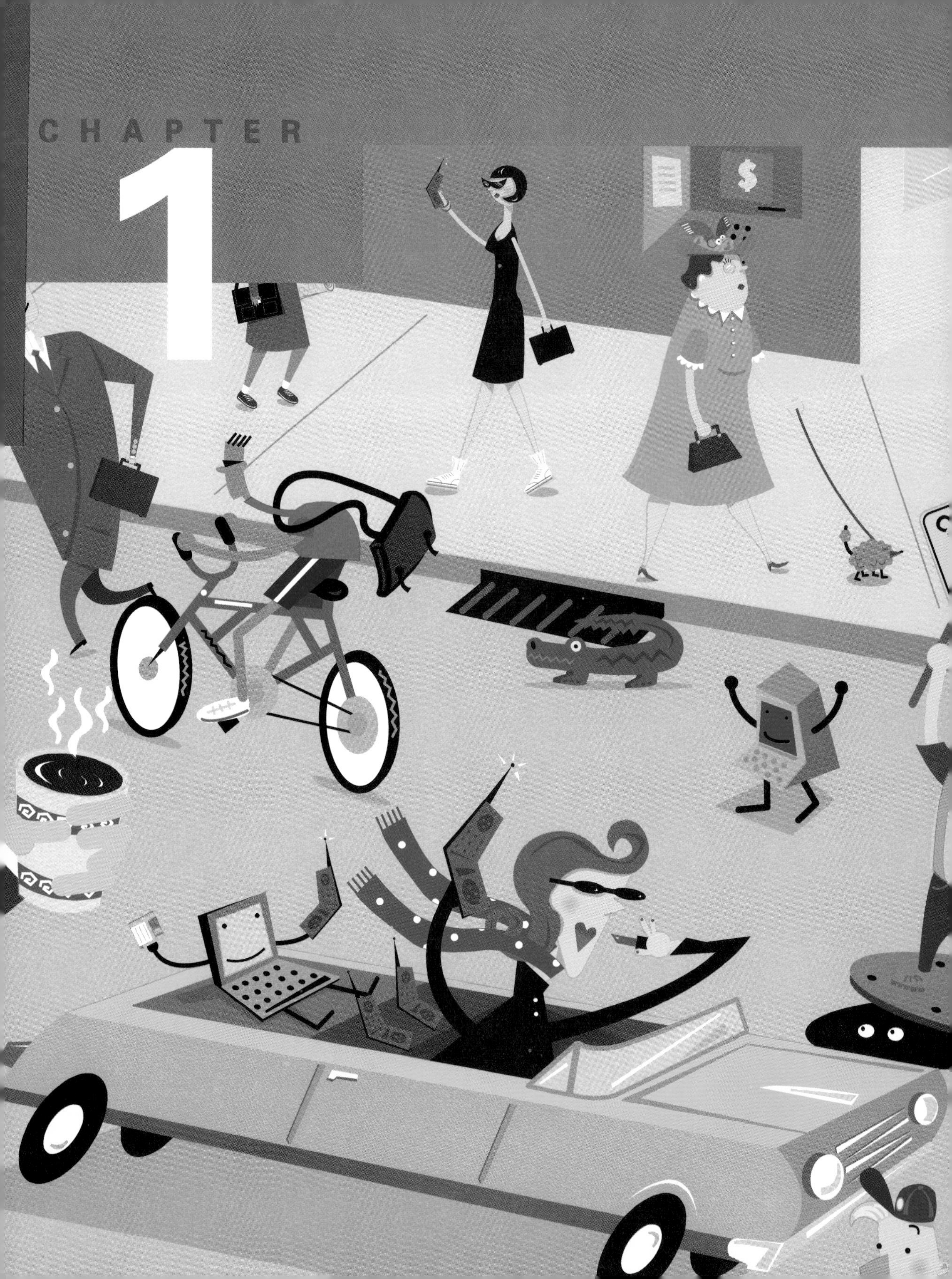

# Getting Started

# FAST FORWARD

## START EXCEL ➤ *pp 7-8*

- Start Excel either by clicking the Start button and choosing Excel from the Programs submenu, or by clicking the Excel icon in the Microsoft Office toolbar.
- You can also launch Excel by double-clicking any spreadsheet file that is Excel-compatible (assuming that you've associated that file type with Excel, of course).

## SELECT CELLS ➤ *pp 8-9*

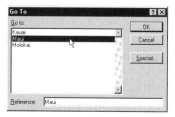

- Click in a cell to make it the active cell.
- Click and drag to select a range of cells.
- Click row or column headings to select entire rows or columns.
- Click the Select All button (above the Row labels) to select all cells.

## NAVIGATE IN WORKSHEETS ➤ *pp 10-11*

- Click worksheet tabs to bring the desired worksheet forward.
- Use the scroll bars at the right edge and bottom of your screen to scroll in Excel worksheets.
- Use the navigational keys (PGUP, PGDN, etc.) to navigate via the keyboard.
- Use the Go To command on the Edit menu (CTRL-G) to reach specific named items.
- Use the Special button in the Go To dialog box to find specific elements (notes, formulas, etc.).

## ENTER TEXT ➤ *pp 11-12*

- Any non-numeric, non-datelike characters that you enter into a cell are treated as text.
- To enter text in a variety of adjacent cells, select the cells first, then tab from cell to cell.
- To force entries beginning with numbers to be displayed as text, change the cell format to text. (Curiously, formulas will still treat the entries as numbers, so be careful!)

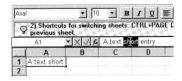

# EDIT TEXT ➤ *p 12*

1. Select the cell containing the text.
2. Modify the text in the Formula bar.
3. Click the check mark button in the Formula bar or press ENTER to save the changes.
4. Click the X (or Cancel) button to discard changes.

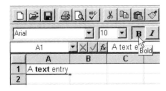

# FORMAT TEXT ➤ *p 13*

1. Enter and spell-check the text.
2. Choose different fonts and type sizes from the Format Cells dialog box reached via the Format menu, or use the Format toolbar.
3. Use the formatting buttons on the Formatting toolbar for Bold, Italic, etc.
4. Use the AutoFormat command on the Format menu if you want Excel to do the formatting for you. (See Chapter 5.)

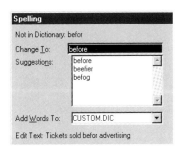

# CHECK SPELLING ➤ *pp 14-15*

1. Finish and proofread your entries.
2. Choose Spelling from the Tools menu or press F7.
3. Accept or reject suggested spelling changes.
4. Save the worksheet after correcting it.

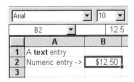

# ENTER AND FORMAT NUMBERS ➤ *pp 16-19*

- Any entry that begins with a number, dollar sign, plus sign, minus sign, or open parenthesis will be considered a number.
- You can enter commas and percent signs when entering numbers, or better still, format cells with desired number format first.
- To enter numbers in a variety of adjacent cells, select the cells first, then tab from cell to cell. When you reach the last selected cell, you will be bounced to the first selected cell in the next row.

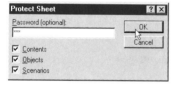

## ENTER FORMULAS ➤ *pp 19-21*

1. Always begin entering a formula by typing an equal sign (=).
2. Build formulas by typing cell references and operators, or with a combination of typing and clicking.
3. Finish formula entries by clicking the check mark button in the Formula bar, or press ENTER.

## COPY FORMULAS ➤ *pp 30-31*

1. Be sure your original formulas contain absolute and mixed addressing where necessary (described in this chapter).
2. Select the cells to be copied, then drag the fill handle, or use the Edit menu's Copy and Paste commands or their keyboard equivalents (CTRL-C and CTRL-V). You can also use the Edit menu's Fill commands when appropriate.
3. Check your work.

## PROTECT YOUR DOCUMENTS ➤ *p 33*

Use the Protection command on the Tools menu to specify the desired levels of protection and passwords for the security features.

## QUIT EXCEL ➤ *p 34*

Use the Exit command on the File menu to quit Excel. You'll be prompted to save any unsaved work.

**I**'ve created and handed out perhaps a thousand spreadsheets in my harried life. Some of the most memorable include detailed construction budgets for a new, multi-million dollar manufacturing building. At about the same time, I created sales forecast worksheets for the very same company that wanted to erect the new factory. *Those* spreadsheets told us that we should *not* invest in a new building. We decided to believe the construction budget and not the sales forecast. The building was built. It came in on time and on budget. A year later, the glass-and-concrete-shrine-to-optimism was sold at auction (because my sales forecast was as accurate as my construction forecast). Good forecasting, bad decision-making. Human error.

Another set of spreadsheets led to my opening a nearly disastrous small business of my own because of—you guessed it, bad forecasting. I employed the same spreadsheet program I used in the corporate setting, took the same basic steps, but used bad assumptions and made bad decisions. Fortunately, other spreadsheets I created in my bedroom/world headquarters that year let me spot the problems in time. I was able to make the necessary changes, and my home business grew and prospered.

The lesson should be obvious. Spreadsheets are just fancy replacements for pencils, paper, and erasers. Without your good judgment and common sense, they just kill trees and distract you from your real mission. But with a little love and care, they can save your butt.

In this chapter, you'll get a review of spreadsheet basics. Then we'll move along to the stuff busy people crave. Excel offers an incredible collection of timesaving features. They are all worth knowing. And remember, when you find yourself doing something over and over, wondering if there is a better way, there probably is. Watch the TipWizard and check online help as you explore.

**habits & strategies**

*Excel has a TipWizard feature that actually watches you work and makes timesaving suggestions. Get into the habit of reading the wizard's advice. (Chapter 2 tells you how to turn it on if it isn't already enabled.)*

# CONCEPTS AND TERMS YOU NEED TO KNOW

Just in case you've been stuck on Gilligan's Island for the past two decades, I'll mention that spreadsheet programs like Excel enable you to create and quickly perform "what-if" analysis of complex, inter-related columnar reports. Excel organizes your prestidigitation into files called *books* containing *worksheets* or *spreadsheets*. (Let's use the terms "spreadsheet" and "worksheet" interchangeably in this book, okay?) Figure 1.1 shows a typical Excel worksheet.

As you know if you've ever created a worksheet before, they are made up of *cells* arranged in *rows* and *columns*—rows run across your screen and columns run down. Books are simply collections of related

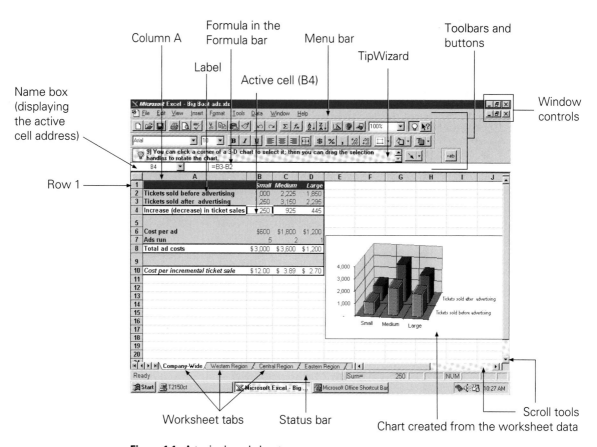

**Figure 1.1**  A typical worksheet

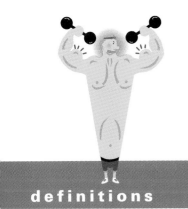

**definitions**

**Formula:** *A collection of instructions Excel uses to compute results.*

**Function:** *Built-in formulas for complex computations like finding square roots and solving engineering problems. See Chapter 7 for details.*

worksheets. You type or otherwise enter things like labels, numbers, and dates into cells. Excel rows are usually identified with numbers, and columns with letters. The *address* of a cell is a combination of the row and column labels. Thus, cell B4 would be the fourth cell down in the second column from the left of the worksheet.

You must also create *formulas* (sometimes called *equations*) in some cells. For instance, you might enter numbers (a.k.a. data) in cells B2 and B3, then place a formula in cell B4 that adds those two numbers and displays the results in cell B4. You can see an example of a formula in Figure 1.1.

Excel also provides tools, menu choices, and functions you can employ to create and use complex formulas. Excel's formatting features let you change the overall appearance of your final work product. And the *Chart Wizard* quickly converts your worksheet numbers and cell labels into impressive pie charts, line graphs, bar charts, three-dimensional charts, scatter charts, etc.

# GETTING STARTED

The obvious way to start Excel is to choose it from the Program submenu of the Start submenu. Or, if you installed Excel as part of Microsoft Office, you can click the Excel icon in the Office shortcut bar. You can also double-click the Excel icon in Windows Explorer, but this takes longer. Starting in any of these ways opens a new, untitled workbook. You can also start Excel by double-clicking Excel worksheet icons and related files. This starts the program and displays the worksheet whose icon you clicked.

The best way to learn Excel is to use it. If you haven't already done so, start the program. You should see a blank worksheet and a new workbook.

## Page Setup First

Since Excel can show you page endings, as well as how much information will fit on each page as you work, it's a good idea to make Page Setup decisions right when you start a new project. Use the Page Setup command located on the File menu. Page size, orientation, and header and footer dimensions are just a few of the things you can control with Page Setup. For your first project you may want to stick

*Did you know that an Excel worksheet is 256 columns wide and 16,384 rows long, containing a total of 4,194,304 cells? How's that for useful cocktail party trivia?*

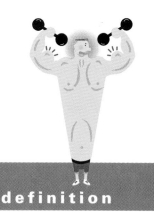

**Range of cells:** *Any two or more cells used together, be they adjacent or not.*

with Excel's default settings, but as a rule you should get in the habit of changing Page Setup settings when you start new worksheets.

The tabs on the Page Setup dialog box will remind you of others that you've seen, except you'll be given choices like printing gridlines, the printing order of pages in reports that won't fit on one page, and so on.

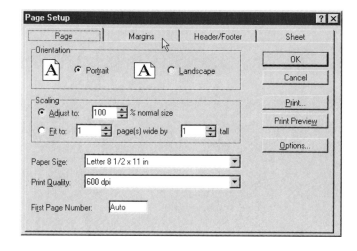

# SELECTING CELLS

Before entering or editing cell contents, or before you can format or move cells, you need to select cells. You can select single cells or ranges of cells.

## Selecting Cells with a Mouse

To select a single cell, simply point and click in it. It becomes the active cell. The following techniques, illustrated in Figure 1.2, are for selecting rows, columns, and ranges.

- Click on a row number to select the whole row.
- Click and drag to select a range of cells.
- Point to a column heading to select an entire column of cells.
- Click on the Select All button at the top-left corner of the workbook to select the entire worksheet.

To select non-contiguous (non-adjacent) cells or groups of cells, hold down the CTRL key and do any of the aforementioned selection

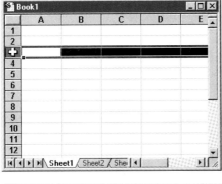
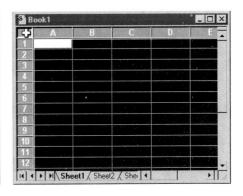
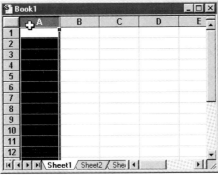

**Figure 1.2** Selecting ranges of cells

tricks. For example, to select rows 2 and 4 but not row 3, click on the number for row 2, then press CTRL while clicking on 4.

## Selecting Cells with Your Keyboard

While you will probably want to use your mouse for most selections (it's quicker), there are many keyboard selection tricks.

- If you've already selected a range of cells, SHIFT-SPACEBAR selects the entire row or rows in which the cells are located.
- CTRL-SPACEBAR selects an entire column.
- CTRL-SHIFT-SPACEBAR selects the entire worksheet.

To *extend* selections in any direction, hold down the SHIFT key and press the appropriate arrow key. The other navigational keys can be used to extend selections also. For instance, SHIFT-CTRL-END extends the selection to the end of your worksheet.

# NAVIGATING WITH THE MOUSE AND KEYBOARD

Most "Windows" keyboard navigational tools work in Excel. For example, you can scroll with the scroll bars, and use PGUP, HOME, and related keys.

| Keys | Action |
|------|--------|
| PGUP or PGDN | One screen up or down |
| ALT-PGUP or ALT-PGDN | One full screen right or left |
| CTRL-PGUP or CTRL-PGDN | One sheet right or left |

The Edit menu offers a number of other navigational aids. For instance, there is a Find command that will remind you of Word's Find command—it lets you search for text strings, formulas, and other items of interest. You can name areas of your spreadsheet by choosing Insert|Name|Define, then you can use the Go To command to quickly find them.

## Navigating with the Go To Command

The Edit menu's Go To command can be used to find areas you've named, or just to go to a specific cell address. This makes it easy to jump around in large sheets. For instance, I've named three data entry areas in the sample worksheet, and these names appear in the Go To dialog box.

**SHORTCUT**

*Click on the active cell address at the left end of the Formatting toolbar and type the desired address. You'll be whisked right to it.*

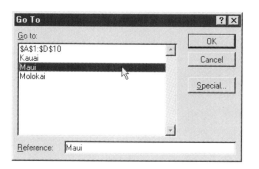

You'll learn more about naming ranges in Chapter 6. For now, it's enough to be aware that it is both possible and handy to be able to name selected parts of a worksheet.

### The Go To Special Button

The Go To Special dialog box (reached by choosing the Special button in the Go To dialog box) lets you select cells meeting specific criteria. For instance, you can specify all notes, formulas, blank cells, the last cell, etc. To inspect only a certain range of cells, first select only the cells of interest before using the Special button. To search the entire worksheet, select any single cell before using the button.

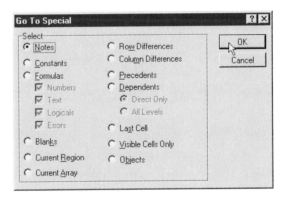

**habits &
strategies**

*When entering text and numbers into a range of cells, if you select the cell range first, you can tab from cell to cell. When you reach the rightmost selected cell, you'll bounce to the leftmost cell in the row below. This eliminates a ton of pointing and clicking.*

# ENTERING AND EDITING TEXT

To enter the text used to label things in your worksheets, simply activate the cell where you want the text to appear (point to it and click), then begin typing. (When you enter text into a cell this way, the text is sometimes referred to as a *constant value*, since you want it to remain the same until you change it yourself.)

As you start typing, the text will appear in the active cell *and* in the Formula bar. Pressing ENTER or clicking the check mark button in the Formula bar concludes the text entry and places the text in the active cell. By the way, pressing ENTER makes the cell below the current cell the new active cell, while pressing TAB moves you to the right, and clicking the check mark button keeps the current cell active. If you change your mind before you finish an entry, you can press the ESC key or click on the X button in the Formula bar to cancel the entry. Figure 1.3 illustrates this.

You can type up to 255 characters per cell. After you've entered text, you can easily increase cell sizes later or word-wrap text to accommodate the entries, as you'll see in a moment. By the way, just

Click to cancel entry    Click to accept entry

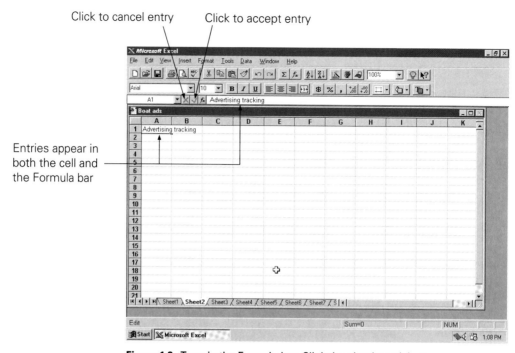

Entries appear in both the cell and the Formula bar

**Figure 1.3**  Type in the Formula bar. Click the check mark button or press ENTER to accept the entry; click the X button or press ESC to cancel

because text spills over into the next cell doesn't mean it lives there. The *entire entry* resides in the cell where you've typed it.

## Editing Text

If you spot an error while entering text, simply backspace to correct it. If you see an error after finishing the entry, activate the cell and edit the text—you can do this by double-clicking in the cell itself or by clicking the cell once and visiting the Formula bar.

Use your Windows text-editing skills here: Drag over the text you want to delete or correct, or double-click to select a word, or select characters using the keyboard. Move the insertion point around in the text on the Formula bar as necessary. When the corrections have been made, press ENTER or click the check mark button.

## Replacing Text

If you activate a cell containing text, then type new text and press ENTER or click the check mark button, the new text will replace the old text.

# Formatting Cells

You can change the appearance of both text and numbers in cells (make things bold or bigger, change fonts, and so on). Normally, all the text in a cell is affected, but you can choose to modify only portions by selecting them.

Use the buttons on the Formatting toolbar, and additional choices reached through the Cells command on the Format menu. The process of embellishing cell appearance is described in more detail in Chapter 5.

# TEXT BOXES

Besides typing text into cells, you can create *text boxes* and place them anywhere you like on your worksheets. They are a kind of graphic object. It's even possible to rotate text in text boxes, and draw arrows from text boxes to the things the text describes. To create a text box, click the Text Box button, then drag your mouse to create a box of the desired size. Release the mouse button and type. You'll learn more about text boxes later in this chapter.

# TEXT NOTES

Text notes are used to hold "pop-up" notes that only appear on your worksheets when you request them. The notes are attached to cells, and can be viewed onscreen by yourself or coworkers. They can also be printed.

# Creating Notes

To create a note, start by selecting the appropriate cell. Then choose Insert|Note or press SHIFT-F2. Excel will display the Cell Note dialog box.

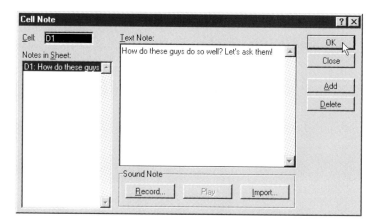

Type the note in the Text Note box. Click Add or OK to attach the note to the cell. A red dot appears in the top-right corner of a cell that has a note attached to it.

## Displaying and Printing Notes

When you hover the mouse pointer over a red dot, the note will appear. Oddly, this does not work if the cell is the active cell. Another way to display (and edit) notes is to select the cell of interest, then press SHIFT-F2. You'll see the Cell Note dialog box.

To print notes, visit the Page Setup dialog box, click on the Sheet tab, and select the Note option box. Turn on the Row and Column Headings option to print cell references with notes.

## Sound Notes

If you have a multimedia-equipped computer, you can record and play back audio notes by using the Sound Note buttons in the Cell Note dialog box. Yeah, but so what? Well, you could conceivably leave "voice mail" regarding a cell using this feature, but only if everyone using the worksheet has multimedia-savvy computers.

# CHECKING SPELLING

Once you've entered the worksheet headings and other text (like chart labels), the Spelling command on the Options menu will launch the spelling checker, as will the spelling button on the Standard toolbar. Besides checking for misspellings, the checker looks for repeated (duplicate) words.

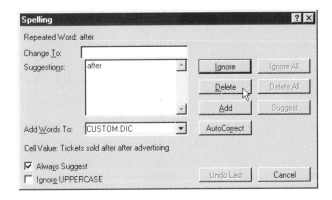

## SHORTCUT

*The F7 function key runs the spell checker.*

# Running the Spelling Checker

To check the spelling of your entire worksheet, run the spelling checker *without selecting a range of cells*. This checks labels, cell notes, embedded charts, text boxes, headers, and footers. It does *not*, however, check text created by formulas.

To check a small portion of the worksheet, select the appropriate range of cells. To check a single word, highlight it in the Formula bar and run the checker.

You can accept Excel's spelling suggestions, ignore them, type your own changes, or add words to the custom dictionary as you do in Word.

# UNDOING AND REPEATING ACTIONS

The Edit menu contains Undo and Repeat commands similar to Word's. There are also the familiar Undo and Redo buttons on the Standard toolbar.

Usually, if you catch a mistake, a trip to the Undo command or use of the CTRL-Z shortcut will fix it. The Repeat command was designed to duplicate your last action. If your last act was to undo something, you can even undo the Undo. On the Edit menu, the exact names of the Undo and Repeat commands change, based on your prior actions—for example, they may say Repeat Paste and Undo Paste. Sometimes you'll see gray "Can't Undo" or "Can't Repeat" commands, indicating that

Excel is unable to undo or repeat your most recent type of operation, at least under the current circumstances.

# ENTERING AND FORMATTING NUMBERS

Numbers are often referred to as *constant values*, or simply *values*. You type numbers into the active cell by using either the number keys above the letter keys on your keyboard, or by using the numeric keypad in NumLock mode. Pressing the NUMLOCK key toggles the numeric keypad between number and cursor-movement mode.

In addition to the numerals 0 through 9, you can enter the following special symbols when typing numbers:

```
+ - ( ) , . $ % E e
```

Excel ignores the plus sign in numeric entries, and considers a number to be negative if you precede it with a minus sign or hyphen or enclose it in parentheses. It treats commas and dollar signs correctly, and accepts numbers entered in scientific notation (2.5E+2, for instance).

When you enter dollar signs, percentages, or commas, Excel changes the number's format.

## Number Formats

Within limits, Excel stores and calculates numbers at the precision you type them, but may display them slightly differently than you typed them. For instance, if you type

**3.141592654**

in a cell, that's what will be *stored* in the cell even if you *see* something else. For example, if you place that entry in a narrow cell, you might see 3.141593. In this case, Excel displays the number at the maximum possible precision under the circumstances and rounds it up to display it. The actual appearance of the number changes with the Number format defined for the cell. (Normally, this affects neither the value itself nor other computations based on the number.)

You can control the precision with which numbers are displayed. All new worksheets start out with all of their cells formatted in General format, which attempts to show as much precision as possible. You

**habits & strategies**

*If you know which cells are going to be used for specific types of numbers you can preformat the cells so that the numbers look right as soon as you enter them.*

can force cells to use other formats designed by Microsoft, or you can create your own formats.

Sometimes, the entry techniques that you use change the cell's Number format automatically. For example, if you activate a cell in the General format, then type a number with a dollar sign, the cell's format will change from General to a currency format.

Typing a percent sign changes a cell's Number format to a percentage with two decimal places (10.05%, for instance). There are scientific and fractional number formats as well. You can specify the Number format for a cell or group of cells from the Number tab in the Format Cells dialog box, shown here. Reach it from the Cells command on the Format menu.

**habits & strategies**

*A quick way to increase or decrease the number of displayed decimal places is to use the buttons called Increase Decimal and Decrease Decimal. They are located on the Formatting toolbar and contain zeros, decimal points, and arrows. Each time you click, display precision is incremented or decremented one decimal place.*

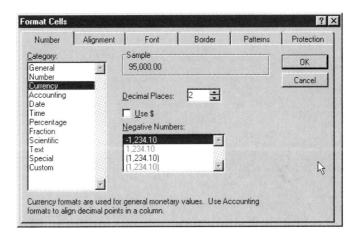

## When Numbers Are Too Big for Their Cells

When a number is too big to be properly displayed in its cell, Excel often displays a series of pound signs (######) instead of the number. Other times, Excel will switch to scientific notation to accommodate a large number.

Making the column wider using techniques described in Chapter 5, or using a shorter number format, will solve the problem. For instance, when dealing with large sums of money, you can often save room in cells by using number formats that don't *display* pennies and decimal points, even if you enter them. They will still calculate correctly.

# Entering and Formatting Dates and Times

You enter dates and times by typing them in most commonly accepted American formats. These include, but are not limited to:

> 08/21/47
> 21-Aug-47
> Aug 21, 1947
> 8:15 PM
> 8:15:15 PM
> 20:15
> 20:15:15
> 08/21/47 20:15

You can even create your own date formats. Excel will *store* entries like these as dates or times, and then *reformat* and *display* them using one of several predefined date formats.

## How Excel Stores Dates and Times

Date and time entries are a slightly confusing topic, made tougher by Excel's desire to be all things to all people. If you ever plan to enter dates into cells, you should know the following.

Excel is often required to do date-and-time math (determine the number of days between two dates, or the number of hours between two time entries, for instance), so it *stores* dates and times as *serial numbers* using January 1, 1900, as the starting date. Here's how it works.

The serial number 1 represents January 1, 1900; the serial number 2 stands for January 2, 1900. If you *reformat* a cell containing a date and display it as a number, you will see the serial number instead of the date. Excel will still treat the cell's contents as a date for computations (but the cell will *look* strange to you).

## Forcing Numbers to Be Treated as Text

If you want Excel to treat numbers or time entries or datelike entries as text instead of numbers, you need to tell it to do so. Suppose, for instance, you want to enter the part number **12/63**. Excel would try to treat this as a date, and instead of seeing your part number in the cell you'd see Dec-63 after you finished the entry. To prevent this, precede such entries with ' (the apostrophe or single quotation mark),

**CAUTION**

*Not all computers use 1/1/1900 as the starting point for their date serial numbers. For example, Excel for Macintosh computers use 1904. Excel usually converts dates from Macintosh spreadsheets properly when importing and exporting, but check carefully when moving worksheets containing dates from one platform to another.*

which will not display or print. Alternatively, since Excel treats any cell containing non-numbers as text, the entries #12/63, 12/63B, and even numbers preceded by a space ( 12/63) will be treated as text.

# ENTERING AND EDITING FORMULAS

Formulas are where the rubber meets the road. When you want to add a column of numbers and see the results, or divide one number by another, or do any other computation, you must create formulas. Formulas are sometimes even used to manipulate text in worksheets.

Usually, you place the formula in the cell where you want to see the results. You type formulas in the Formula bar. Excel formulas always start with = (equal sign), although die-hard Lotus users can cheat and use + (plus sign) instead.

Remember the sample advertising cost worksheet shown in Figure 1.1? It contains formulas to compute the costs of obtaining new customers through advertising.

**SHORTCUT**

*AutoCalc even lets you total the numbers without having to create a formula. Read about AutoCalc in Chapter 3.*

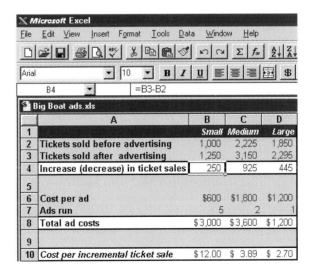

The increased unit ticket sales formula in cell B4 subtracts the preadvertising tickets sold (located in cell B2) from the tickets sold after advertising (in cell B3) to compute and display the improvement. Notice that the formula does this by referring to the two cell addresses B3 and B2. Whenever the contents of B3 or B2 change, Excel will automatically

## habits & strategies

*Excel's TipWizard just reminded me that the shortcut for displaying and hiding formulas is* CTRL-`*. That's* CTRL *plus the grave accent mark, usually located on the same key as the ~ (tilde) symbol. It toggles between displaying formulas and their answers.*

compute a new answer and display it in cell B4. That's the essence of worksheet computations! Formulas tell Excel what to do whenever the contents of specified cells change.

Use the View tab in the Tools|Options dialog box to show all of your worksheet's formulas at once:

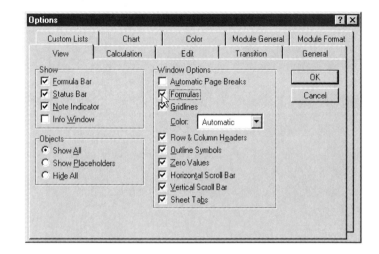

# Creating Formulas

Start by activating the cell where you want to place the formula (click on B4, for instance). Next, type either an equal sign or a plus sign to tell Excel you want to create a formula.

You can then either type the formula one character at a time, or *assemble* it using your mouse and keyboard. For instance, you could type **=B3-B2** and press ENTER to create the formula in B4—but it's often better to reach for the mouse. You could type the equal sign, then point to and click on cell B3 with your mouse. Cell B3 will be surrounded by a dashed outline (I like to call this "the marching ants"). The cell's address will appear in the Formula bar. This makes it unnecessary for you to *type* the address with the keyboard. Next, you'd type the minus sign for your equation, then point to and click on cell B2 with the mouse. Pressing ENTER finishes the formula. If you have entered values in cells B2 and B3, the value in B2 will be subtracted from the value in B3, and their difference appears in cell B4.

# Excel's Formula Operators

The *operators* you use in a formula tell Excel what you want to do (add two numbers, or compare things, for instance). For purposes of explanation, Excel operators can be divided into four general categories—*arithmetic*, *comparison*, *text*, and *reference*. Most of the time you will use arithmetic operators. The others can be useful for more complex projects.

## Arithmetic Operators

You've already seen arithmetic operators at work—the plus sign (+), for example, and the minus sign (–). Here's the standard collection:

| | |
|---|---|
| + | addition |
| – | subtraction |
| * | multiplication |
| / | division |
| % | percentage |
| ^ | exponentiation |

Simply include these at the appropriate places in your formulas to perform the desired calculation. For instance, the formula =B5*10% would compute 10% of the contents of cell B5. The equation =B5^2 computes the square of cell B5's contents.

More complex formulas, like

=E6*B2–(B3*10%)

can be created by combining operators and using parentheses. (Recall your algebra lessons or see the section in this chapter titled *Order of Evaluation in Formulas* to learn more about parens.)

## Comparison Operators

Comparison operators let you inspect two values and come to a conclusion about their relative values. They are usually coupled with Excel's *logical functions* (discussed in Chapter 7).

The operators are:

| | |
|---|---|
| = | equal to |
| > | greater than |
| >= | greater than or equal to |
| < | less than |
| <= | less than or equal to |
| <> | not equal to |

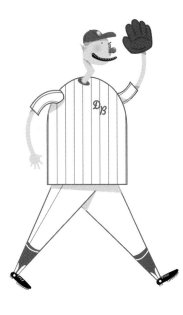

## Text Operator

Excel's only text operator is the ampersand (&). It is used to combine text. For instance, if you had the word "cow" in cell C7 and the word "boy" in C8, the formula =C7&C8 would create the text string "cowboy".

## Reference Operators

Finally, Excel offers reference operators. The most common reference is to a range of cells. For instance, the expression B1:C3 refers to cells B1, C3, and all the cells between them. In other words, you use colons to separate the first and last cell addresses in a cell range. You'll learn more about ranges later in this chapter.

# REFERENCING CELLS

When creating a formula, you will frequently refer to a *single cell*. Other times it is useful to refer to ranges of cells. In an annual budget, you might have 12 different cells, each containing totals for a different month. It's possible to refer to individual cells or all of the cells in the range.

You often specify references by clicking or dragging with your mouse (clicking on cell A1, or dragging from cell B1 to B4, for instance). Alternatively, you can type references directly into formulas (like A1 or B1:B4). When you create and duplicate formulas, Excel makes some assumptions about which cell or cells you wish to reference. You can often overrule these assumptions as you'll see in a moment. References can be *absolute*, *relative* or *mixed*. Let's consider a simplified budget exercise designed to illustrate various reference types and referencing techniques.

| | A | B | C | D |
|---|---|---|---|---|
| 1 | Proposed budget increase | 10% | | |
| 2 | | | | |
| 3 | | | | |
| 4 | Item | Last Year | This Year | Next Year |
| 5 | Radio | $ 525,000 | $ 600,000 | $660,000 |
| 6 | Travel magazines | $ 50,000 | $ 70,000 | $ 77,000 |
| 7 | Handbills | $ 6,000 | $ 1,000 | $ 1,100 |
| 8 | Total | $ 581,000 | $ 671,000 | $738,100 |
| 9 | | | | |
| 10 | 3 Year non-radio costs | $ 205,100 | | |

# Single-Cell References

Single-cell references specify a particular cell. For instance, when building a new formula, if you wanted to include the 3-year non-radio costs from our example, you could either click upon cell B10, or type **B10** in the new formula. An important variation on this technique creates absolute references, and will be discussed momentarily.

# Range References

To refer to a range of cells, you can either drag over the desired cells, or type the beginning and ending cell addresses in the range, using a colon to separate the beginning and ending cell addresses. For instance, to specify the group of six cells containing non-radio costs in our example, you would either drag from cell B6 to D7 or type **B6:D7** into your formula. Incidentally, you can give *names* to ranges of cells and refer to the names in equations. For instance, you could name cells B6 through D7 *NonRadio* and place the range name "NonRadio" in your formulas. This approach often makes it easier to understand and troubleshoot complex worksheets. Read more about this technique in Chapter 6.

# Absolute vs. Relative References

Sometimes you'll want to specify an exact cell not only for the first formula you create, but for others that will be modelled after it. This is particularly important when building formulas that you plan to copy. (In case you don't already know, creating a "master" formula and copying it repeatedly whenever you need it can save you a lot of time, as you will see momentarily.)

Suppose, in our example, we want to create a formula that increases radio advertising expenses by a specified percentage over

**SHORTCUT**

To reference an entire row, type its number twice, separated by a colon (2:2, for example). To specify an entire column, type the column's letter twice with a colon (A:A, for instance).

last year's spending. We could just include the cell address containing the percentage increase (B1) in our formula:

| | A | B | C | D |
|---|---|---|---|---|
| | | D5 | ▼ ✕ ✓ ƒₓ =(C5*B1)+C5 | |
| 1 | Proposed budget increase | 0.1 | | |
| 2 | | | | |
| 3 | | | | |
| 4 | Item | Last Year | This Year | Next Year |
| 5 | Radio | 85000 | 95000 | =(C5*B1)+C5 |
| 6 | Travel magazines | 12000 | 17000 | =(C6*1)+C6*B1 |
| 7 | Handbills | 0 | 1500 | =(C7*1)+C7*B1 |
| 8 | Total | =SUM(B5:B7) | =SUM(C5:C7) | =SUM(D5:D7) |
| 9 | | | | |
| 10 | 3 Year non-radio costs | =SUM(B6:D7) | | |
| 11 | | | | |

This would work fine until you tried to save some time by copying the formula for other rows using the techniques later in this chapter, or rearranged the worksheet. While *copying* the formula, Excel would increment (adjust) the reference to B1 as shown here. Thus the first formula will work and the others won't because they refer to cells other than B1:

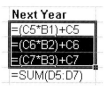

| Next Year |
|---|
| =(C5*B1)+C5 |
| =(C6*B2)+C6 |
| =(C7*B3)+C7 |
| =SUM(D5:D7) |

**SHORTCUT**

*To change a reference to absolute, place the insertion point just after the cell address and press F4.*

You'll learn more about this when you learn to duplicate formulas later, but here's the solution if you are familiar with the problem and just can't wait. To assure that formulas always refer to a specific cell (like the one containing the mark-up percentage in our example), it is wise to make an *absolute* reference. Absolute addresses use dollar signs before both the row and column address. For instance, to create an absolute reference to cell B1, you would type **$B$1**.

## Mixed References

Finally, it is worth mentioning that you can create mixed references that point to a specific column and a relative row (like $A1), or a specific row and a relative column (like A$1), or a specific worksheet and relative row and column. Again, this will make more sense when you start copying formulas.

# Named References

You can assign names to cells or ranges of cells. When you do that, you can use the names in your formulas. For instance, if you had a column named QTY and a column named Price, you could create a formula like =QTY*PRICE. Read more about this in Chapter 6.

Naturally, you can edit the reference by typing in a formula directly (to add or remove dollar signs, for instance). But here's an alternative.

## EDITING REFERENCES IN A FORMULA step by step

1. Select the cell containing the formula to be changed.

2. In the Formula bar, select (or just click at the end of) the reference to be changed (B1, for example).

3. Press F4 repeatedly, watching the reference change until you see the desired effect ($B$1, for example).

4. Press ENTER or click the Enter button (the little check mark button in the Formula bar) to change the formula.

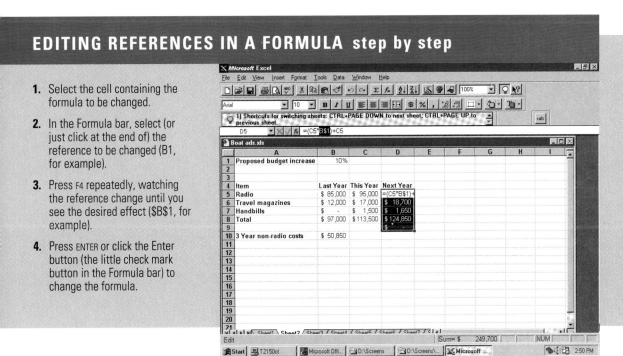

# Changing Reference Style

By default, Excel uses letters for column references and numbers for row references (A1 for instance). It is possible, however, to use "R1C1" style referencing, as shown in the next illustration.

| R5C4 ▾ | | =(RC[-1]*R[-4]C[-2])+RC[-1] | | |
|---|---|---|---|---|
| | **1** | **2** | **3** | **4** |
| **1** | Proposed budget increase | 10% | | |
| **2** | | | | |
| **3** | | | | |
| **4** | Item | Last Year | This Year | Next Year |
| **5** | Radio | $ 85,000 | $ 95,000 | $ 104,500 |
| **6** | Travel magazines | $ 12,000 | $ 17,000 | $ 17,000 |
| **7** | Handbills | $ - | $ 1,500 | $ 1,500 |
| **8** | Total | $ 97,000 | $ 113,500 | $ 123,000 |
| **9** | | | | |
| **10** | 3 Year non-radio costs | $ 49,000 | | |

Notice that there are numbers both for columns and rows. Inspect the formulas in the example as well. When you choose this option, Row references in formulas must be preceded with the letter "R" and Column references with the letter "C."

This is a method used in some competitive spreadsheet programs like MultiPlan, so if you find it easier to use (or if your organization has standardized on this method), it's easy to change over to this reference style.

1. Choose Tools and then Options.
2. Bring the General tab foremost if it is not already in view.
3. Choose R1C1 on the Reference Style area of the dialog box.
4. Click OK. Excel will adjust all of your formula references automatically.
5. To switch back to "normal" Excel referencing, repeat steps 1 through 4, choosing A1 in step 3.

# ORDER OF EVALUATION IN FORMULAS

Whenever you add more than one operator to a formula, Excel must decide which *operation* to perform first. Moreover, the *position* of the elements in your formula play a part. For example, the formula =5+2*10 yields 25, while =10*5+2 yields 52; this makes sense when you understand the order in which Excel performs operations. In the first example, Excel adds five to the product of 2 times 10. In the second example, 10 is multiplied by 5 and its product (50) is added to 2, since addition occurs after multiplication in the order of evaluation. Here's a list of Excel's operators in the order Excel uses them:

| Operators | Function |
|---|---|
| : | Range specifiers |
| (space) | Intersection (see online help) |
| , | Union |
| – | Negation (creating a negative number by using only one operand) |
| % | Percent |
| ^ | Exponentiation (raising to a power) |
| * or / | Multiplication or division |
| + or – | Addition or subtraction |
| & | Joins text |
| = < > <= >= < > | The comparison operators |

As you may recall from algebra class, you can often use parentheses and other tricks to force the correct order of evaluation. For instance, =10*(5+2) returns 70 (not 52 as it does without the parens).

# Built-In Functions vs. Hand-Built Formulas

Excel provides a number of built-in functions that automate otherwise time-consuming common tasks. For instance, there is a function that computes monthly loan payments given a loan amount, interest rates, and the length of your loan. Another function computes averages for specified groups of numbers. Other functions perform engineering or statistical tasks. There is also a Function Wizard to help you sort out all the details. You'll learn more about functions in Chapter 7. But there is one worth learning about now. It's called the SUM function, and it can be reached with the AutoSum button on the Standard toolbar.

Suppose you wanted to add the first column of numbers in Figure 1.4. You *could* type the equation:

**=A4+A3+A2+A1**

Functions make quick work of laborious tasks like adding rows or columns of numbers.

**habits & strategies**

*If you just need a quick sum, and don't particularly need to have it appear in your worksheet, Excel has a new AutoCalc function that calculates the sum of any numbers selected and places the result in the status bar. See Chapter 3 for details.*

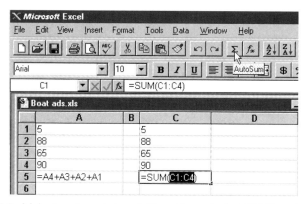

**Figure 1.4**  A laborious formula in cell A5 and its equivalent SUM function in C5

As you can see in column C of Figure 1.4, the SUM function is a better way to get the sum of those figures. When I created this figure, I made C5 the active cell and pressed the AutoSum button, which caused Excel to enter the name of the function (SUM) in the Formula bar and propose arguments for the function (in this case, cell addresses). In Figure 1.4, Excel proposes the cell range C1 through and including cell C4. "Marching ants" surround the cells to be included.

The SUM equation also appears in the Formula bar, where you can accept or edit it. Pressing ENTER or clicking on the Formula bar's check mark button will accept the proposed formula and display the answer in cell A6. The AutoSum button and related SUM function work on rows, columns, or arrays (described next).

## Arrays and Formulas

Formulas can include references to *arrays*, which are contiguous (adjacent) groups of numbers. For instance, if you wanted to sum the cells B2:C5, you might type **=sum(** then drag to select the cells in the array, then press ENTER to finish the formula.

## LOOKUP TABLES

Lookup tables are special arrays that you create to help you look up and provide different cell contents as conditions warrant. For instance, you could create a lookup table like the one in cells A3 through B5 here:

*Lookup tables need not be on*

*the same page or even the same*

*sheet with the cells containing*

*lookup formulas. Consider*

*putting your lookup tables*

*out of sight.*

*You've just read about the essentials of*
*table lookups. Consult the big books*
*and online help for more information.*

| B10 | ▼ | =LOOKUP(A10,$A$3:$B$5) | | |
|---|---|---|---|---|
| **A** | **B** | **C** | **D** | **E** |
| **1** | | | | |
| **2** Guests | Rate | | | |
| **3** 10 | $14.95 | | | |
| **4** 25 | $ 10.95 | | | |
| **5** 50 | $ 7.75 | | | |
| **6** | | | | |
| **7** | | | | |
| **8** 10 | 14.95 | | | |
| **9** 100 | 7.75 | | | |
| **10** 25 | 10.95 | | | |
| **11** | | | | |

The lookup table itself consists of the range of cells A3:B5. Cells A3 through A5 contain quantities for each of three price breaks. Cells B3 through B5 contain the prices.

To demonstrate a lookup table at work, there are identical sample formulas in cells B8, B9, and B10. (The formula for cell B10 is shown in the illustration. It was created using the Insert Function command and the resulting Function Wizard.) You'll learn more about this in Chapter 7.

Cells A8 through A10 contain different numbers of guests. As you can see from the illustration, the LOOKUP functions in the formulas places the appropriate price in cells B8 through B10 based on the quantities entered in cells A8 through A10. You can specify exact lookups or have Excel find the closest match as illustrated in this example.

Incidentally, you can use lookup tables with text as well as numbers. Here, Excel inserts different words based on order quantities. All I did was replace the cell *contents* in B3, B4, and B5 with text:

| B9 | ▼ | =LOOKUP(A9,$A$3:$B$5) | | |
|---|---|---|---|---|
| **A** | **B** | **C** | **D** | **E** |
| **1** | | | | |
| **2** Guests | Rate | | | |
| **3** 10 | Small group | | | |
| **4** 25 | Medium group | | | |
| **5** 50 | Large group | | | |
| **6** | | | | |
| **7** | | | | |
| **8** 10 | Small group | | | |
| **9** 100 | Large group | | | |
| **10** 25 | Medium group | | | |
| **11** | | | | |

## Controlling Recalculation

Normally, Excel recalculates each time you change any number in the worksheet. And, unless you instruct it otherwise, Excel always recalculates before saving. To overrule these automatic recalculation options, choose Tools|Options, select the Calculation tab, and then select the Manual option.

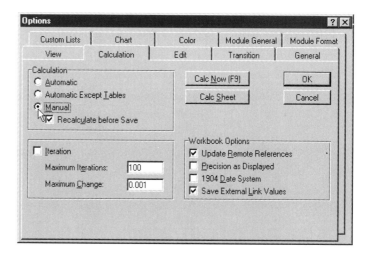

When working on large, complex projects, consider shutting off automatic recalculation if lengthy recalculation delays bother you. Just remember that once you disable automatic recalculation, you become responsible for telling Excel when to recalculate. If you make changes to your worksheet and forget to recalculate manually, one or more cells containing equations may contain old, incorrect answers. To recalculate the worksheet manually, press F9. Stick a note on your monitor to remind you to recalculate before you save the worksheet, or use the Recalculate before Save option.

**SHORTCUT**

*The traditional Windows keyboard shortcuts for copying and pasting (CTRL-C and CTRL-V) work for copying Excel formulas.*

# COPYING ENTRIES AND EQUATIONS TO MINIMIZE TYPING

When creating a large worksheet it is time-consuming to type the same values over and over and over again. Why do it when Excel can do this for you? And, when creating similar formulas in different cells, sometimes the only things that change in the formulas are cell references. For instance, if you create an equation like =A1-A2 in column A, you often want similar equations like =B1-B2 in column B and =C1-C2 in column C.

Excel provides a number of powerful features to minimize mindless typing like this. But you need to use these power tools with care!

## Copying and Pasting Formulas

One way to copy formulas is to select them and use the Copy command on the Edit menu, then select the cell first destined to get a copy of the formula and press ENTER. Excel will attempt to alter the cell references in your formulas to accommodate the request. In cases where you've copied multiple cells, you'll need to make sure there are enough blank (or at least "disposable") cells to receive the new formulas.

## Copying Formulas with the Fill Handles

Frequently, an easier way to copy formulas to adjacent cells is to select the original cell and drag the fill handle (the little black box at the lower-right corner of the selected cells) to copy the formula.

| Edit | |
|---|---|
| Undo Column Width | Ctrl+Z |
| Can't Repeat | Ctrl+Y |
| Cut | Ctrl+X |
| Copy | Ctrl+C |
| Paste | Ctrl+V |
| Paste Special... | |
| Fill | ▶ |
| Clear | ▶ |
| Delete... | |
| Delete Sheet | |
| Move or Copy Sheet... | |
| Find... | Ctrl+F |
| Replace... | Ctrl+H |
| Go To... | Ctrl+G |
| Links... | |
| Object | |

|  | ▼ |  | =A1-A2 | |
|---|---|---|---|---|
|  | **A** | **B** | **C** | **D** |
| **1** | 100 | 60 | | |
| **2** | 20 | 40 | | |
| **3** | 80 | | | |
| **4** | | | | |

# SAVING AND RECALLING WORKSHEETS

Excel uses the Windows 95 standard Save, Save As, and Open procedures. It supports long filenames. Figure 1.5 shows a typical Save As dialog box.

Excel's default file extension is .XLS, so you won't need to type it. By default, Windows 95 does not display file extensions, but they are there, and can be displayed if you like. See my book *Windows 95 for Busy People* (Osborne/McGraw-Hill, 1996) to learn how.

## upgrade note

*If you use Excel's new long filename feature, remember that users in your organization with older versions of Excel (and Windows) can't see the long filenames you've assigned to your files. Consult Windows 95 books like my* Windows 95 for Busy People *to learn how to work around this.*

Choose a destination computer, drive, or folder from this list

Click Save to save your work

Choose a destination folder from this list

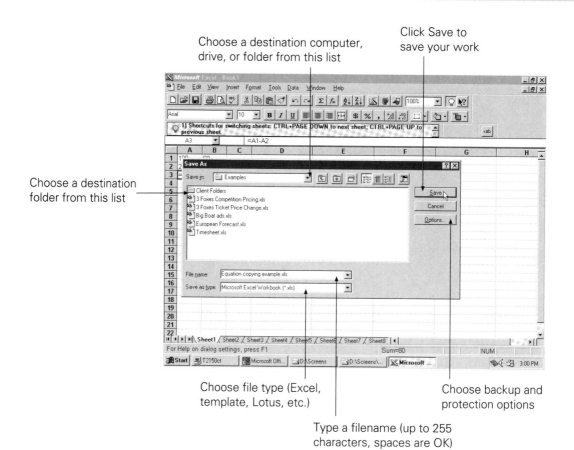

Choose file type (Excel, template, Lotus, etc.)

Choose backup and protection options

Type a filename (up to 255 characters, spaces are OK)

**Figure 1.5** The Save As dialog box

# PREVENTING OTHERS FROM OPENING YOUR DOCUMENTS

To restrict access to your worksheets you can assign passwords that prevent people from opening your files without a password. Alternatively, you can let people open but not change your worksheets, or you can let them open the file and have Excel recommend that they not change it. This is all done by clicking the Options button in the Save As dialog box and assigning passwords.

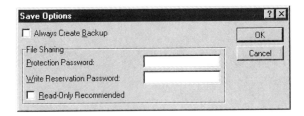

# PROTECTING CELLS

It is also possible to protect cells in your worksheets. This is particularly useful when others use your worksheets, but I, for one, protect a lot of my personal files to safeguard myself from myself (or is that my evil twin brother who's always replacing formulas with numbers?).

When you turn on the Protect Sheet option, all of the cells in your sheet are protected. So to protect some cells and not others, you need to turn on the Protect Sheet feature, and remove protection from the cells that you want people to be able to change. It's a little confusing, but, in any event, here are the basic steps for protecting cells:

1. Select the cells you wish to unprotect (places where you want to enter variables—numbers, names, etc.).
2. Choose Cells from the Format menu.
3. Click the Protection tab in the Format Cells dialog box.
4. Click to remove the check from the Locked box and click OK.
5. You must turn on protection by visiting the Protection command on the Tools menu and choosing either Protect Sheet to protect only the current sheet or Protect Workbook to protect the entire workbook.

6. Enter an optional password in the resulting dialog box.

7. Re-enter the password to prove that you were paying attention the first time, and click OK (capitalization counts).

8. To unprotect the work, use the Unprotect command on the Tools menu. You'll need to provide the correct password if you or someone else originally specified one.

# QUITTING EXCEL

To quit Excel, choose Exit in the File menu, or double-click the Close box in the very top-right corner of your screen. (Or you can pull the plug on your computer, but that's a really bad idea.) When you ask to quit Excel properly, you will be reminded to save any unsaved work first.

# WHERE DO WE GO FROM HERE?

Well, busy person, now you know enough to be dangerous. You can try a few projects on your own at this point, or read a little longer. I vote for the latter approach since the next two stops (Help and Timesaving Tips) might save you hours of frustration.

MAIL

# Getting Help

# FAST FORWARD

## HOVER THE MOUSE POINTER FOR HELP ➤ *p 40*

To see the name of many onscreen objects:
1. Slide the mouse pointer over the object (a button, for instance).
2. Leave it there for a moment.
3. The item's name will often appear.

## START ONLINE HELP ➤ *pp 40-41*

Choose Microsoft Excel Help Topics from the Help menu or press F1 with an Excel window active.

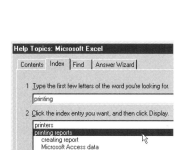

## USE HELP'S FIND TAB ➤ *pp 41-43*

1. Choose Microsoft Excel Help Topics from the Help menu or press F1.
2. Click the Find tab if necessary to bring it forward.
3. Type word(s) of interest.
4. Double-click a topic in the resulting list.
5. ESC closes the Help window.

## USE HELP'S INDEX TAB ➤ *p 45*

1. Choose Microsoft Excel Help Topics from the Help menu or press F1.
2. Click the Index tab if necessary to bring it forward.
3. Type word(s) of interest.
4. Double-click a topic in the resulting list.
5. ESC closes the Help window.

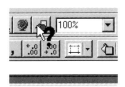

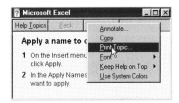

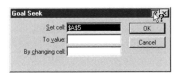

## USE HELP'S CONTENTS TAB ➤ *pp 46-47*

1. Choose Microsoft Excel Help Topics from the Help menu or press F1.
2. Click the Contents tab if necessary to bring it forward.
3. Double-click a book.
4. Double-click pages when you see them.
5. ESC closes the Help window.

## GET "WHAT'S THIS?" HELP ➤ *p 48*

1. Click the little question mark box in the upper-right corners of most Excel windows (or the bigger one on the Standard toolbar).
2. The mouse pointer shape changes.
3. Point to an object of interest.
4. Click on unknown devices (buttons, sliders, etc.).
5. Read the resulting text.
6. ESC closes the Help window.

## PRINT HELP TOPICS ➤ *p 48*

1. Make sure your printer is ready.
2. Bring up a Help topic.
3. Click the Options button.
4. Choose Print Topic.
5. Click OK.
6. Press ESC to close help window.

## GET HELP IN DIALOG BOXES ➤ *p 48*

Many Excel dialog boxes contain small Help buttons containing question marks. Clicking these buttons and pointing to objects in the dialog box frequently provides useful help. For example, clicking the Help button and clicking on the Set Cell box in the Goal Seek dialog box will provide information about the Set Cell box.

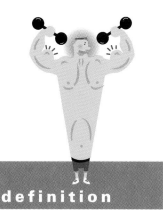

**definition**

*Wizard: Problem-solving programs that launch, seemingly by themselves, while you are working with Windows and other Microsoft programs. Wizards ask you multiple-choice questions and then either fix problems, change settings, or tell you something. They can even help create specialized worksheets.*

*With so much online help available these days, it is sometimes easy to get confused. There's Windows 95 online Help, and Excel online Help, and the TipWizard. Unless otherwise indicated, the Help feature or menu that we are referring to in this chapter is Excel Help, not Windows Help.*

**E**xcel provides very powerful online help features. For instance, you have just seen in the Fast Forward section how hovering your mouse pointer over things often displays their names. In a moment you'll learn about a huge library of indexed help text and how to search it. Excel also provides an Answer Wizard and a TipWizard. Some of the help you'll receive is based upon observations Excel makes about the way you work. It will even notice your bad habits and suggest better (or at least different) ones.

For tougher problems, Microsoft provides automated dial-up help. You can access it via telephone, fax, or data modem. Let's take a closer look at today's wide array of Excel help options.

## DON'T CONFUSE WINDOWS HELP WITH EXCEL HELP

Windows 95 and Excel both offer help. Sometimes it's easy to get confused. At the risk of oversimplifying this, if your question is about your computer itself (the display, memory, sound, disk drives, etc.) start your journey in the Windows 95 Help system. Windows help is available from the Windows Start menu. Excel help is found on the Help menu located on the Excel menu bar.

If you have questions specific to Excel, try the Excel Help feature. For more obscure problems (like networking maladies, advanced font trivia, and the like, try dial-up resources like the Microsoft Network, Microsoft's WWW site, America Online, CompuServe, etc. These external sources of information are often more current and complete than the Help files shipped with Excel. And don't forget to rub elbows in the various user-to-user areas of these dial-up sites.

## OPENING THE EXCEL HELP WINDOW

Choose Microsoft Excel Help Topics from the Help menu or press F1. You'll see a window like the one in Figure 2.1.

Displays an alphabetical list of Help topics

Lets you search for particular terms and displays found items

Runs the Answer Wizard, an intelligent assistant

Click to see Help topics organized in "books"

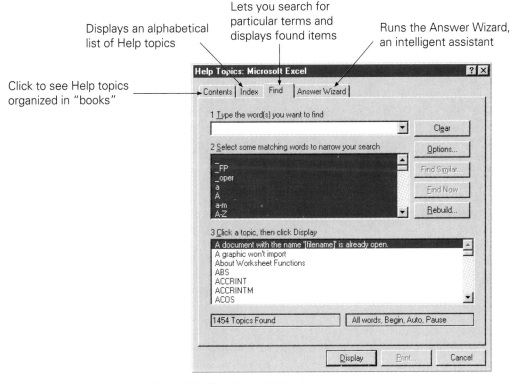

**Figure 2.1** The Excel 7 Help window

With this window in front of you, you can choose to see help organized in "books" (using the Contents tab), or view a list of topics listed alphabetically (via the Index tab), or type a key word or phrase (in the Find tab) and see what happens. Then there is the Answer Wizard tab. It lets you ask "natural language" questions like "Tell me about Page Setup" and get answers or at least a list of related help topics. My personal favorite form of help comes from the Find tab.

# THE FIND TAB

'Spose you want to find out about previewing a worksheet before printing it.

1. Choose Microsoft Excel Help Topics from the Help menu or press F1.

2. Click the Find tab if necessary to bring it forward. (The very first time you do this, the Help software might display a Help Wizard asking you what kind of database you'd like to set up. If this happens, click the Next button, and then Finish.)

3. Type the word or phrase of interest (**preview**, for example).

4. Either scroll through the list of topics and double-click one, or type an additional word to narrow the search. Here, simply typing the beginning of the word print (**pri**) gets you into the right neighborhood:

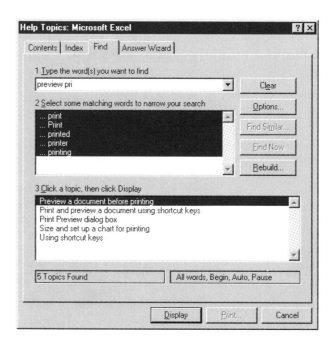

### habits & strategies

*You can frequently leave Help Topics open as you try the prescribed steps. Just drag and perhaps resize the Help window so it fits in some out-of-the-way location on your screen. This eliminates the need to memorize or (gasp!) print.*

5. Double-click the topic, or click once to select, then click the Display button.

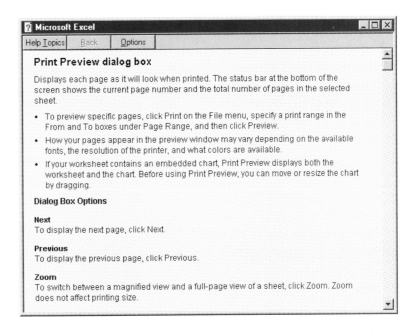

6. Use the Close box or the ESC key to quit Help and get back to work. (Clicking the Help Topics button takes you back to the Find tab.)

# HELP WINDOW TRICKS

Excel Help offers numerous, subtle features that you should not ignore. Here are some of my favorites.

## Buttons in Help Text

Many Help windows contain buttons nestled within the Help text. These provide additional assistance. Some of these buttons run programs, open the control panel so that you can make adjustments, etc. For instance, in the illustration that follows, clicking the tiny button with the arrow on its face will provide different answers based on the symptoms you describe (select).

**habits & strategies**

*Try clicking those tiny buttons*

*when you see them.*

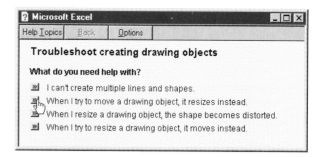

# Highlighted Words Provide Definitions

Clicking the colored, underlined words in Help screens ("fill handle" in this example) provides definitions of the terms.

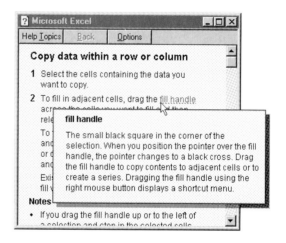

# The "See Also" Notes

To see related Help Topics, click on the colored "See Also" notes found in some Help windows. They will reveal a list of (hopefully) cogent topics. Not all Help windows contain cross-references. But if you are staring at one that does, double-click on a topic, or select it and click the Display button.

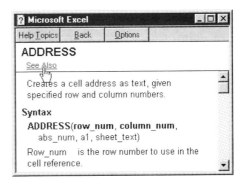

**SHORTCUT**

*You can quickly narrow a search of the index by typing the first few characters of a topic. For instance, typing* **back** *gets you in the "backup" neighborhood.*

# THE INDEX TAB

The Index tab in your Help window provides an alphabetical list of topics. You can scroll the list with the PGUP, PGDN and other navigational keyboard keys, or with the scroll tools and your mouse. Once you spot your topic, double-click it. Follow the steps for using the Index tab as illustrated in the following section.

## USING THE INDEX TAB step by step

1. Choose Help|Microsoft Excel Help Topics or press F1.

2. Click the Index tab.

3. Type the first few letters of the word or phrase of interest.

4. Add more letters to focus the search. (Backspace to delete if the focus is too narrow.)

5. Double-click on the desired topic in the list. (This often produces a new list of topics.)

6. Select a topic from the list, and double-click to read it.

7. Use the Close box or the ESC key to close the Help window.

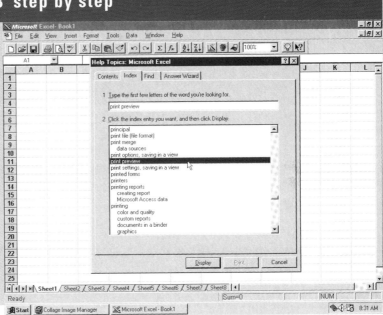

*I never cared for this Contents tab approach—too much double-clicking for me. But try it. You might like it.*

# THE CONTENTS TAB

The Contents tab presents you with tiny icons that look like books. When you double-click these book icons, they reveal additional book icons, and eventually little Help page icons. Double-clicking the page icons brings up Help text to read.

1. Choose Microsoft Excel Help Topics from the Help menu or press F1.
2. Click on the Contents tab, if necessary, to bring it forward.
3. Double-click a book (*Creating Formulas and Auditing Workbooks,* for example).

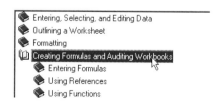

4. Double-click another book (*Using Functions*, perhaps).

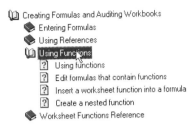

5. Click a topic of interest or scroll to a different book (*Insert a worksheet function into a formula*, for example) and double-click there.

6. Double-clicking on pages (icons) with question marks displays the Help topic:

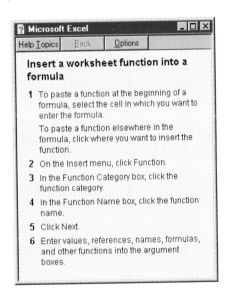

7. Read, and perhaps print the topic.

8. To learn more, click on any buttons or colored words (like definitions) you might find in the Help topic.

9. Use the Close box or the ESC key to quit help. (Clicking the Help Topics button takes you back to the Contents tab.)

# PRINTING AND COPYING HELP TOPICS

You can print Help topics once you have them on your screen. Make sure your printer is ready. Click the Options button in the Help window's button bar. Choose Print Topic. Make any necessary changes in the resulting Print dialog box (number of copies to print, etc.) Click OK or press ENTER to start printing.

# "WHAT'S THIS?" HELP

Do buttons leave you clueless? Have you always wondered what that little puffy button above the row label is for? The next time you see a gizmo that is not self-explanatory, look to the upper-right corner of the Excel parent window (in the Standard toolbar) for a little button with a question mark like this one.

When you see the Help button:

1. Click it.
2. Your mouse pointer's appearance will change. (It gets a little tag-along question mark of its own.)
3. Point to the source of your confusion.
4. Click.
5. You will probably get an explanation.

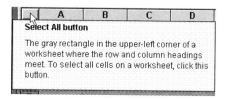

6. Clicking a second time turns off "What's This?"

# DIALOG BOX HELP

Occasionally Excel will ask you a bizarre question or make some disturbing proclamation. If the dialog box causing the interruption contains a Help button (which should not be confused with the Help button in the Standard toolbar), give it a click. Sometimes you'll get useful assistance.

# THE ANSWER WIZARD

The Answer Wizard is Microsoft's most recent attempt at commercializing artificial intelligence. The results are, well...artificial. In theory, you simply type natural language questions (English, for example) and the Wizard either tells you what you want to know, or shows you how to do what you want done. Sometimes the cranky old wiz will just do what it thinks you want done. Here's an example. Suppose I want to know how to print only selected cells. I might choose Answer Wizard from the Help menu and type the question "**How do I print selected cells**?"

Much of the wiz's "natural language" is mythology. It looks for key words of interest and displays a variety of possible topics from which you pick. For example, entering either the full sentence or the two key words just mentioned causes the wizard to display this set of Help topics:

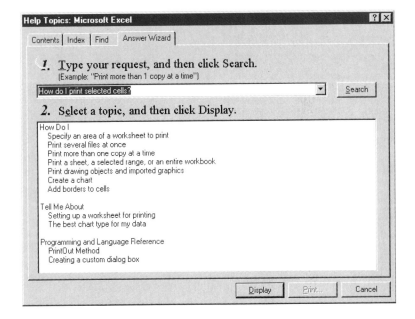

Since the closest-sounding topic is "Specify an area of a worksheet to print," double-clicking it will cause the wizard to literally demonstrate the process, as shown in the next illustration.

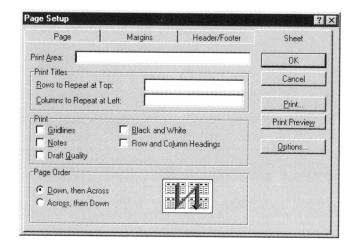

The wiz will visit the File menu for you, choose the Page Setup command and open the dialog box, then post a little note of explanation. Clicking removes the note but leaves the dialog box where you can do what you were told to do, or you can press ESC to leave things alone and quit the Help exercise.

The wizard is an amazing, entertaining, and sometimes frustrating pet. The results will vary based on how you phrase the question and how the wizard was programmed to respond to key words in your phrase. And, of course, human language is full of ambiguity, which confuses the heck out of computers. For example, a search for help with absolute references (as opposed to relative references) is likely to also turn up information about cell reference types (A1 vs. R1, C1).

# THE TIP WIZARD

The TipWizard—get this—watches you work and displays suggestions in the Toolbar. After you get over the ego problems associated with machines knowing more than their owners, the TipWizard is a godsend. It might be the busy person's most important Excel tool. Here, the TipWizard is telling me the keyboard shortcut for making characters bold, since it is quicker to use the shortcut than it is to visit the Format menu (which it noticed I just did for purposes of this TipWizard demonstration).

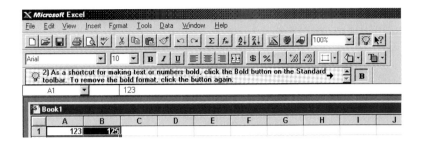

## Turning the TipWizard On and Off

Usually the TipWizard is on the job, and the light turns yellow when there is a new tip. If you want to turn the TipWizard off, click the TipWizard button to make the wizard's toolbar disappear. Clicking the button a second time makes the wizard's toolbar reappear.

# HELP FOR LOTUS 1-2-3 USERS

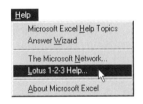

If you've grown up around Lotus 1-2-3, Microsoft has been kind enough to offer help designed to rid us of those—how shall I say this?—bad habits of ours. Lotus 1-2-3 Help is an installation option, and if it was not installed, you will need to visit the Windows 95 Control Panel and use the Add/Remove Software feature to add Lotus 1-2-3 Help with the Microsoft Excel (or Microsoft Office) Setup program's assistance. Once 1-2-3 Help is installed, it appears on the Help menu. Choose it to get the help you need.

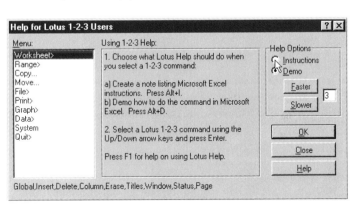

# DIALING UP THE MICROSOFT NETWORK FOR HELP

If your computer is modem-equipped, and if you have set up your Microsoft Network account, you might find the help you need in Microsoft's Knowledge Base, or perhaps in the User-to-User areas.

# USING MICROSOFT'S FAST TIPS SERVICE

Microsoft provides 24-hour-a-day, 365-day-a-year technical support via fax and prerecorded voice tips. You access these tireless slaves from any touch-tone phone, fax, or modem. Since all busy people have fax machines, I assume you do too:

1. From any phone (it need not be your fax phone), dial (800) 936-4100 for help with Excel and other desktop applications (Word, etc.). You can now use this same number to reach support for Microsoft Office and Windows 95-related trouble.
2. Listen to the choices.
3. Use your phone's touch-tone pad to request a "map" or catalog of available documents and recordings.
4. Enter your fax telephone number when prompted to do so. (Be sure the fax machine or modem is ready to receive.)
5. When you have been told that the document will be faxed, hang up and watch another tree fall on your behalf.
6. Call back with map in hand and request the desired information.

# OTHER SOURCES OF AUTOMATED HELP

There are perhaps a thousand or more online sources of Windows 95 and Windows application-related help. Many of these resources provide lists of other places to graze. Table 2.1 lists a few to get you started. Just remember. No overnight camping. You are busy!

| Resource | Reach via | Notes |
|---|---|---|
| Microsoft Knowledge Base and Software Library | America Online, CompuServe, The Microsoft Network, Microsoft's WWW site (see below), and others | An amazing collection of tips, work-arounds, bug reports, files, and more. |
| Microsoft's Worldwide Web Server | **http://www.microsoft.com/** | Where do you want to go today? Even job postings here! |
| Users Groups | The Computing sections of America Online, CompuServe, Prodigy, and others. (Many neighborhood users groups have their own BBSs too.) | Don't confuse the experts with the wannabe experts. Advice in these groups runs the gamut from brilliant to dangerous. |

**Table 2.1**  Dial-up Help Resources

To learn more about outside sources of help, type **technical support** in the Find tab of the Help dialog box and double-click the topic Connect to Microsoft technical resources. Click on the various buttons to learn more.

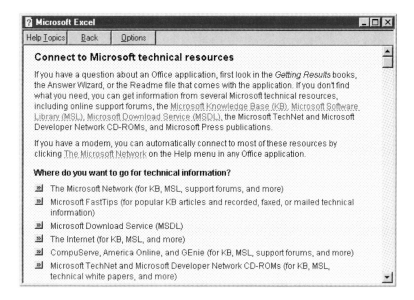

# Timesaving and Customizing Tricks

INCLUDES

- Using and creating templates

- Changing Excel's default settings

- Using AutoCalculate, AutoFill, AutoComplete, and AutoFilter

- Spell checking

- Utilizing toolbars and buttons

- Personalizing toolbars

- Applying keyboard shortcuts

# FAST FORWARD

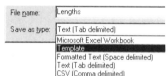

### USE MICROSOFT TEMPLATES ➤ *pp 59-67*

1. Install the optional, preformatted Microsoft templates when you set up Excel, or use the Add/Remove Programs feature on the Windows Control Panel to add them later.
2. To load a template for a specific problem (loan analysis, time-keeping, etc.), choose the New command in the File menu.
3. Click the Spreadsheet Solutions tab.
4. Double-click the icon for the desired template.
5. Enter your data (variables).
6. View, test, and print the results.
7. Save the finished project as a regular Excel workbook if you like. (By default, Excel saves your results in a workbook.)

### CREATE YOUR OWN TEMPLATES ➤ *p 67*

1. Open a new workbook.
2. Create worksheets and test them carefully.
3. Choose Save As in the File menu.
4. Choose Template from the Save as type list.
5. Specify a folder location and filename for the template. (Put Excel templates in the Templates folder or its subfolders.)
6. Click OK.
7. When you next need the template, its icon can be found in the New dialog box's Spreadsheet Solutions tab.

### CHANGE EXCEL'S DEFAULT SETTINGS ➤ *pp 67-68*

1. To change the default workbook and worksheet settings (like fonts, page layout, etc.) create an *autotemplate*. Start by creating a worksheet with the desired settings.
2. Choose Save As on the File menu.
3. Locate the XLStart folder in the Excel folder.
4. Choose Template in the Save as type list.
5. Name the file Book.xlt.
6. Confirm the replacement of the old file Book.xlt.
7. Click OK.

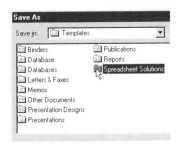

# SPECIFY THE TEMPLATE'S
# TAB LOCATIONS ➤ *p 67*

To ensure that templates show in the proper tab in the New dialog box:

1. Create and test the template.
2. Choose Save As from the File menu and specify template (*.xlt) in the Save as type list.
3. Locate the Templates folder (in the Excel or Office folder).
4. To place templates in the Spreadsheet Solutions tab, save the template in the Templates folder. To have the template appear in a different tab, select the corresponding subfolder (either Spreadsheet Solutions or a subfolder you created yourself) in the Save As dialog box.
5. Click Save.

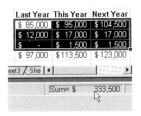

# SEE QUICK COMPUTATIONS
# WITH AUTOCALCULATE ➤ *pp 68-69*

1. Select the cells of interest.
2. Look at the AutoCalculate area of the status bar at the bottom of the screen to see the sum of the selected cells.
3. To view averages, counts, min, max, etc., right-click the status area and pick the desired option.

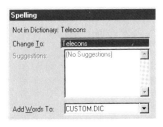

# SPEED WORKSHEET CREATION
# WITH AUTOCOMPLETE ➤ *pp 69-70*

- AutoComplete watches the first few letters you type in a cell and attempts to complete the cell entry based upon other things you've typed previously.
- To see and pick from a list of possible cell entries based on other words you've typed in the current column, right-click the cell and choose Pick from List.

# GET IT SPELLED RIGHT WITH
# AUTOCORRECT AND SPELL CHECKING ➤ *pp 71-72*

1. After making all spreadsheet entries, activate cell A1 and press F7.
2. The spell checker will search for unrecognized words and display the first one found along with a suggested spelling. Unless you've turned off AutoCorrect, it will automatically correct typos as you type.
3. Click OK to accept the suggestion and continue, Ignore to leave the spelling as is, etc.

## CUSTOMIZE TOOLBARS ➤ *p 73*

1. Right-click a toolbar.
2. Choose Customize on the shortcut menu.
3. Click buttons in the dialog box to read about them.
4. Drag buttons from the dialog box onto your toolbar.

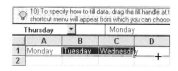

## SPEED NEW PROJECTS WITH AUTOFILL ➤ *pp 74-76*

- AutoFill will automatically extend a series when it recognizes one. For example, if you type Monday in cell A1 and Tuesday in A2, selecting those two cells and dragging will automatically enter the remaining days of the week in order.
- AutoFill also recognizes and can extend months, years, and date combos such as Mon-Yr, for example.
- AutoFill can extend a linear series of numbers as well. For example, typing, selecting, and dragging 10 and 20 will produce 30, 40, etc.

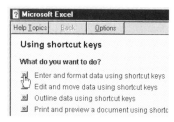

## LEARN KEYBOARD SHORTCUTS ➤ *p 76*

1. Choose the Index tab in Excel Help.
2. Type **keyboard**.
3. Double-click Keyboard Shortcuts.
4. Double-click Using shortcut keys.
5. Click the topic of interest.
6. Use the Back button if necessary to retrace your steps.

**D**on't you just hate repetitive grunt work? Nothing is more frustrating than realizing you've done similar spreadsheets from scratch a few dozen times. You can be much more productive than that! In this chapter, you'll read about Excel's template feature—a powerful variation on the old save-and-reuse technique. You'll learn how AutoCalculate can give immediate answers to many math questions without resorting to formulas. And you'll see how AutoComplete can cut your typing time considerably. Excel's spelling checker is described here too, as is AutoFilter, a great way to find specific data of interest. Finally, don't miss the information on customizing your toolbars and keyboard shortcuts. Let's get to it!

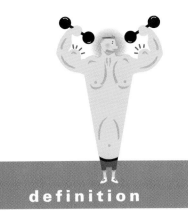

**definition**

*Template:* A worksheet (or workbook) containing labels, equations, and other elements designed to solve a specific problem. Users simply enter variable data and view or print the results. If someone else makes the template, you can at least share the blame for wrong answers.

# USING AND MODIFYING TEMPLATES

Microsoft and Village Software in Boston, Massachusetts have created a series of worksheet solutions for everyday problems. With these templates you can find out how much your loan payments will be if you buy a new car or home. You can create invoices for your company, plan a personal budget, and more. Open a template, enter your information, and when you save your work, it is saved as a regular workbook, so that the template is not destroyed. Excel comes ready to do all this.

Well, I should have said Excel comes *almost* ready, because when you initially set up Excel or Office, chances are only a few of the available templates were installed. To see which Excel templates have been installed on your computer:

1. Launch Excel.
2. Choose New from the File menu.
3. Click the Spreadsheet Solutions tab.

4. If you don't see all of the templates shown in Figure 3.1, you might want to install some or all of them using the steps that follow.

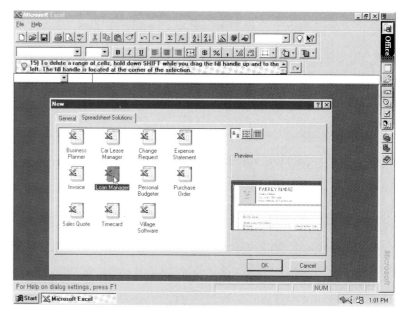

**Figure 3.1** Viewing installed templates

# Installing Optional Microsoft Templates

In case you've forgotten how to add software using Windows 95, here's the short course. To install additional templates:

1. Visit the Windows 95 Control Panel (reached by choosing Start|Settings). Have your installation disks or disc ready.
2. Pick Install/Remove software.
3. Double-click Excel if it is listed, or Microsoft Office if that is the only choice.
4. Click the Add/Remove button.
5. Click Excel, if necessary, to select it.
6. Click Change Option.
7. Click Spreadsheet Templates and then click the Change Option button again.

8. Place check marks next to the desired templates, then repeatedly click OK and Continue as necessary to complete the installation.

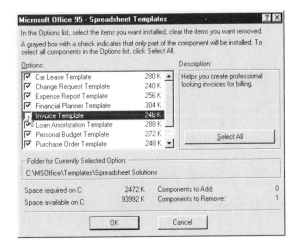

### upgrade note

*Excel 7 offers many more templates than previous versions, and their level of sophistication is much improved. It is worth exploring these Microsoft templates, if only to get design ideas for your own work.*

# Exploring and Using Templates

Once you have the templates installed, they will appear in the Spreadsheet Solutions tab of the New dialog box as illustrated back in Figure 3.1. To preview a template in the little Preview box, click once on the icon for the template of interest. To actually start a new project using a template, double-click its icon. For example, let's look at the Loan Manager template shown in Figure 3.2. It was designed for lending institutions, but you can just as easily use it yourself. You use a template by filling in the missing information and viewing or printing the results.

Notice also that this template and many others contain *multiple worksheets*, indicated by the named tabs at the bottom of the screen

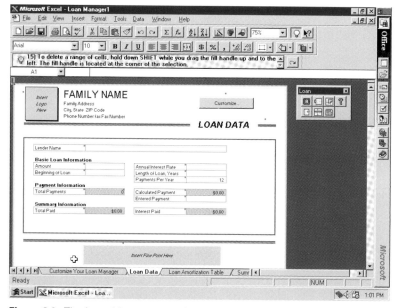

**Figure 3.2** The Loan Manager template

*Read Template Help. Print it out if the information is complex or important. Hover your mouse pointer over cells with CellTips. Read and heed the tips! Be careful not to enter data into cells containing formulas. You might damage the template and get incorrect results.*

(Loan Data, Loan Amortization Table, etc.). Finally, notice that when you opened the template a new toolbar appeared containing seven buttons.

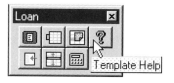

These buttons give you information about the template, toggle the display of sample data, reveal a calculator, and more. Here too, hovering your mouse pointer over the buttons displays their names. Take a moment to click the Template Help button on the Loan toolbar and read about the Loan Manager template. You can print the description and instructions if you like by choosing Print Topic from the Help window's File menu.

You can either modify the appearance of the template (add your own artwork, include "fine-print disclaimers," etc.), or use the template as is. Let's try *using* the template first and change its appearance later.

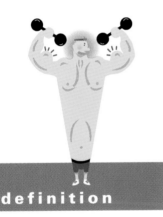

Suppose, for example, that you were considering a new car loan of $25,000 for three years at 9.75%, and that you planned to make monthly payments. Start by clicking the Loan Data tab to select it. You might then click the blank cell to the right of the Amount label and enter **25000**. No need to type dollar signs and commas—Excel will format the number for you. Next, either click or press ENTER to reach the Beginning of Loan blank. Are you confused by the cryptic description of this blank cell? The label cell for the blank cell has one of those little dots. Hover the pointer over the cell and read the resulting CellNote.

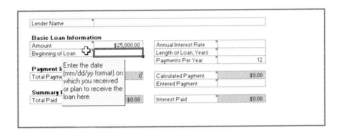

Ah ha. The template needs the date when you plan to drive off in your new car, entered in the format mm/dd/yy.

Don't type in the shaded (green) boxes, as tempting as it is. Instead, skip up to the Annual Interest Rate blank and type **9.75** and move to the Length of Loan, Years blank to enter **3**. Finish by typing **12** in the Payments Per Year blank if it is not already there.

### definition

***CellTips:*** *Little dots (red squares if you have a color display) that tell you to hover your mouse pointer over a particular cell in order to get helpful information about the cell.*

You should see the payment numbers by now. Yikes! Over 800 bucks a month. Try four years. Still too much each month, huh? How about 5 years?

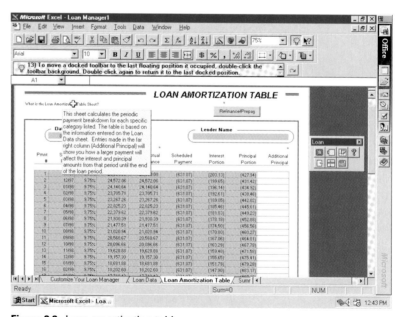

| Lender Name | | | |
| --- | --- | --- | --- |
| **Basic Loan Information** | | | |
| Amount | $25,000.00 | Annual Interest Rate | 9.75% |
| Beginning of Loan | 11/7/97 | Length of Loan, Years | 5 |
| | | Payments Per Year | 12 |
| **Payment Information** | | | |
| Total Payments | 60 | Calculated Payment | $528.11 |
| | | Entered Payment | |
| **Summary Information** | | | |
| Total Paid | #N/A | Interest Paid | #N/A |

This loan is currently too long for the Loan Amort Table. Increase table length to obtain summary information.
The loan table length can be increased to 60 entries on the customize sheet

*As it turns out, you'll be able to amortize five years with this template. Keep reading.*

Whoops. Look at the warning note beneath the Summary information. It's in an unusual spot, but it's important reading. This is what happens when someone else designs worksheets for you. Maybe this version of the template can't accommodate loans of this length. It's hard to tell from that warning note. You can, if you have the time and inclination, figure out what's going on and maybe even redesign the template to accommodate more years. But to prevent getting bogged down here, let's change the number of years back to **4**. Click the Loan Amortization tab and view the table Excel has created, shown in Figure 3.3.

A table which only a banker or a CPA could love. More than you ever wanted to know about your new Jeep's financial future. And best of all, you can "what-if" all day. What if the interest rate is 8%? What

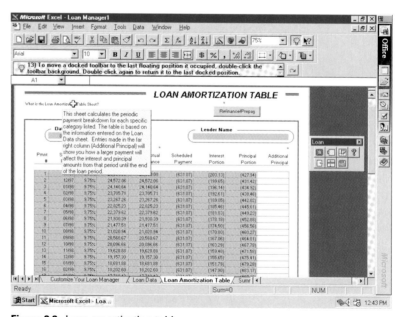

**Figure 3.3** Loan amortization table

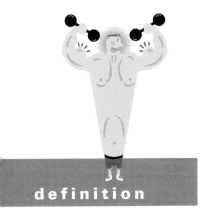

*Scenario Manager: An automated assistant that will run multiple iterations of spreadsheet variables. In the Loan Manager example you could use it to try a variety of interest rates, amounts, periods, etc. Like having your own clerk, only cheaper, and never on vacation.*

*The customizing tab disappears after you've visited it once, but if you click the Customize button on the Loan Manager form, the button will take you to the customizing area.*

if you put more money down? For really big projects with lots of variables, you can employ the *Scenario Manager*, which is discussed in Chapter 11. Ahh. Computers.

# Changing Templates

There are three reasons you might need to change a template: It might be missing important elements like your company logo or name, address, and phone number. Or the template might not compute the things you need computed the way you desire. Or, finally, you might just hate the overall appearance—the typestyles and such.

## Adding Missing Elements

Many templates come with placeholders for things like your name and address, a company logo, disclaimer text, etc. This is stuff you'll probably change once, then resave the template before entering any data so that the elements need only be entered once. For example, I am sure you noticed the placeholders in the Loan Manager template. When you first use the Loan Manager it displays an additional tab called Customize Your Loan Manager. When you click the tab you'll see a "form" into which you can type the necessary personal data. Figure 3.4 shows part of that form.

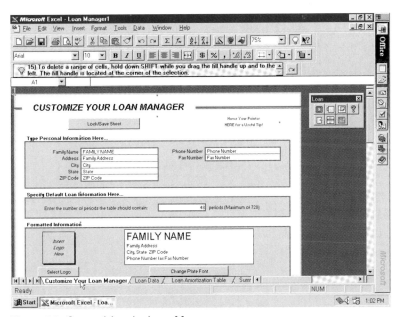

**Figure 3.4** Customizing the Loan Manager

65

*Every protection scheme is different, and just because you can change something in a template doesn't mean you should.*

**habits & strategies**

*Creating good templates is an art and a science. Even moderately complex ones with gee-whiz stuff like the Loan Manager require a programmer's steady hand. You are probably too busy to become a template programmer. Hire one, or use services like Village Software. They do custom work.*

Remember how we couldn't compute loans longer than 48 months a moment ago? Notice that one of the entries in Customize Your Loan Manager tab defines the maximum number of months that can be computed. Simply changing this number will redesign the whole Amortization table without your needing to futz with the formulas. Take your time. Study each available screen when exploring someone else's templates. Look for buttons that simplify the selection and insertion of graphics, and change formulas and typestyles (like the ones in the Loan Manager). These tools can save you time and trouble.

After you've made your changes, many templates (including the Loan Manager) have a button that will save the changes and prevent others from undoing your beautiful creation.

In the case of the Loan Manager, when you click the Lock/Save Sheet button after you've made your changes, you'll be given a chance to just lock, or both lock and save the template *under a new name* so that the old template will remain unscathed and your new one will be personalized and protected. Later, if you want to make changes, use the Unlock This Sheet button that replaces the Lock/Save Sheet button when a template is locked. What a country!

## Changing Formulas and the Design

When you are certain that you've exploited all of the built-in buttons and devices for changing the template's design, you can change formulas yourself. The techniques described throughout this book can be used to alter most templates. For example, the View menu lets you display, inspect, and alter formulas. The Function Wizard lets you insert new functions and so on. Just remember to check your work!

## Changing the Look of a Template

You can, of course, change the color of various art and type elements, fiddle with the size of things, rearrange them, change the names of blanks on forms, etc. Just don't get carried away, and make sure that the changes don't interfere with the operation of the template.

# The Template Wizard

You might have read about a feature called the Template Wizard and hoped it was a gizmo that asked you 20 questions, then developed a template like the Loan Manager. Alas, no. This is a specialized assistant for linking worksheets to databases, particularly in complex

*If you save templates in the*

*Templates folder they will*

*appear under the General tab.*

*You can create your own tabs by*

*creating subfolders and placing*

*templates within the subfolders.*

corporate projects. You are too busy and the pages herein are too few to explore *that* wiz. Leave it to the pros.

# Creating Your Own Templates

On the other hand, anybody can create useful templates. Create an empty budgeting workbook and save it as a template. Put together the elements of a business plan as a template and try it on multiple business ideas. Create your own timesheet template or invoice template if you don't like the ones from Microsoft. Knock yourself out. To save the templates:

1. Create and carefully test a new worksheet or workbook.
2. Choose Save As.
3. Specify a meaningful name (Ron's Time Sheet, for example).
4. Pick Template from the drop-down type list.
5. You will see a choice of template folders in the Save As dialog box. Put that puppy where it belongs by choosing the appropriate folder and clicking Save.

*To go back to using Excel's defaults,*
*delete the Book.xlt file from your*
*XL Start folder.*

# CHANGING EXCEL'S DEFAULTS WITH AUTOTEMPLATE

When you launch Excel it makes some assumptions about the settings for things like fonts, column widths, color patterns, chart types, and on and on. You can change the default settings by creating a template containing the desired settings and giving it a specific name and folder location, as shown in the following steps.

## CHANGING DEFAULT SETTINGS step by step

1. Create a worksheet with the desired settings.

2. Choose Save As on the File menu.

3. Locate the XLStart folder in the Excel folder (which might be in your MSOffice folder).

4. Choose Template in the Save as type list.

5. Name the file **Book.xlt**.

6. Confirm the replacement of the old file Book.xlt if necessary.

7. Click OK.

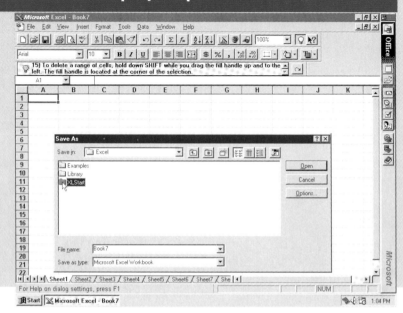

From now on, when you launch Excel it will start with these new settings.

## AUTOCALCULATE

Here's one of those features you'll wish you had in Word and other programs too. It lets you see the sum of a group of numbers by merely selecting them onscreen. With a simple mouse click you can display the average of the selected numbers instead, or count the entries, or find the largest or smallest number. The feature is called *AutoCalculate*.

To use AutoCalculate:

1. Select the numbers of interest.
2. Watch the Status bar. It will display a calculation and the calculation's name (Average, Count, Count Nums, Max, Min, or Sum).
3. To change the type of calculation, right-click the status area containing the calculation and pick the desired calculation type. For example, to display the average of the selected numbers, pick Average.

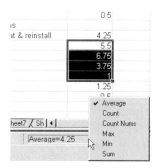

# AUTOCOMPLETE

Wouldn't it be nice to avoid repetitive typing? AutoComplete can really speed up data entry. Consider the small timesheet in Figure 3.5. It contains the names of three different clients, descriptions of work done for them, and the number of hours spent on each task.

Excel "remembers" each of the entries you make in each column. When it comes time to make a new entry in a cell, Excel "watches" you type. When it thinks it recognizes an entry that you've already made *anywhere else in the current column*, it fills in the rest of the characters for you. So, if I typed an uppercase **L** in cell A17, Excel would fill in "askin." Alas, if I type a lowercase **l**, Excel will also fill in "askin," making the entry all lowercase.

There's another potential gotcha worth knowing. One of the "Berger" entries that I manually typed is followed by a space (which you can't see in the example, but trust me, it is there). So, when I type **B**, or **Ber**, or even **Berge**, Excel does not know whether to insert Berger or Berger(space), and it solves this dilemma by entering nada. It's trying to think, and nothing happens. You can avoid this problem by keeping your manual entries consistent.

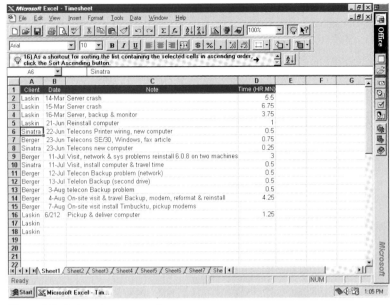

**Figure 3.5** A timesheet example

# AutoComplete Entries from a List

To see and possibly choose an entry from Excel's list of entries for a column, simply:

1. Right-click to activate the desired cell and display the shortcut menu.
2. Choose Pick from list.
3. Point to the desired entry and click to insert it in the active cell.

Incidentally, in the preceding illustration you can see those almost identical Berger entries—one with and one without a space at the end. But ya can't tell which is which. Too bad there aren't little dots to indicate spaces like there are in Microsoft Word, huh?

AutoComplete is an option, and it must be turned on for it to work. (It is on by default.) If you hate it or if it gets you into trouble by entering the wrong things, you can turn it off by choosing Tools|Options|Edit and then selecting or deselecting the Enable AutoComplete for Cell Values check box. Phew!

# SPELL CHECKING

Excel has a spelling checker that will help you ferret out errors in worksheet text, charts, text boxes, custom buttons, headers, footers, cell notes, and the Formula bar. It not only behaves like spell checkers in other Microsoft Office products, it even shares the same custom dictionaries if you have Microsoft Office installed. And, like other newer Office components, Excel provides AutoCorrect, a feature that recognizes and automatically corrects typos.

When you have finished entering text in your worksheet, activate (click on) cell A1 and press the Spelling button in the Standard toolbar, or press F7, or choose Spelling from the Tools menu.

Excel's spelling checker will zip through the entire first sheet and stop whenever it finds a word it does not recognize. You will be given the option of accepting the suggested respelling, ignoring the unrecognized spelling, adding it to your custom dictionary, or setting up an automatic correction for errors that you make repeatedly.

## CAUTION

*Excel only checks the spelling of the current worksheet in multiworksheet books. If you have text on other worksheets, be sure to click their tabs and spell check each sheet.*

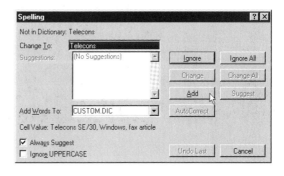

## AutoCorrect

Excel's AutoCorrect feature spots and fixes common typos as you make them—like switching the "e" and "h" when you type "the." To see and possibly modify the list of automatic corrections, visit the AutoCorrect dialog box, reached with the AutoCorrect command on the Tools menu (or with the AutoCorrect button in the Spelling dialog box).

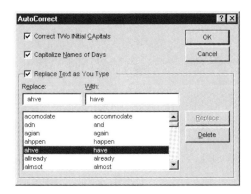

Here you can specify automatic replacements and see previously defined replacements. You can choose other self-explanatory options as well. Visit online help to learn more about the spelling checker (search for "spell") and AutoCorrect.

# USING AUTOFILTER TO FIND SPECIFIC DATA

When you have a worksheet with many, many rows of data, it is sometimes nice to see just the rows meeting a specific criteria. It's easier to understand with an example. Remember the timesheet back in Figure 3.5? There are entries for three different clients. Suppose I only wanted to see the Berger entries. I could use AutoFilter to do that.

1. Activate a cell anywhere in the list of data.
2. Click to choose Filter from the Data menu.
3. Choose AutoFilter from the resulting submenu.
4. Little buttons will appear in each column heading. Click a button to reveal its filter list.

## CAUTION

*When a worksheet is being filtered, not all of the rows are showing. This can cause problems if you are unaware. Check row numbers. If a list is filtered, row numbers will not be consecutive. The triangle in the filter button will change color when filtering.*

5. Choose the entry you wish to display (Berger, for example).
6. Voilà! Just the Berger entries appear.

| A2 | | | Berger | |
|---|---|---|---|---|
| | **A** | **B** | **C** | **D** |
| **1** | Clien | Dat | Note | Time (HR.M |
| **2** | Berger | 23-Jun | Telecons SE/30, Windows, fax article | 0.75 |
| **3** | Berger | 11-Jul | Visit, network & sys problems reinstall 6.0.8 on two machines | 3 |
| **4** | Berger | 12-Jul | Telecon Backup problem (network) | 0.5 |
| **5** | Berger | 13-Jul | Telelon Backup (second drive) | 0.5 |
| **6** | Berger | 3-Aug | telecon Backup problem | 0.5 |
| **7** | Berger | 7-Aug | On-site visit install Timbucktu, pickup modems | |
| **8** | Berger | 4-Aug | On-site visit & travel Backup, modem, reformat & reinstall | 4.25 |
| **17** | | | | |

This same basic approach works with the other columns as well. And instead of displaying specific text entries, you can display rows containing blank cells, or the ten biggest numbers, etc. Experiment. To redisplay all of your rows, choose All in each column list or simply turn off AutoFilter in the Data menu.

# A TOOLBAR TOUR

There are a bezillion toolbar buttons and it would take another book this size to describe them all in detail. But there is a quick way to get to know each toolbar button and its function. When you find buttons you like, it is easy to add them to your toolbars. Come with me.

## CUSTOMIZING YOUR TOOLBAR step by step

1. Right-click in any non-button portion of the toolbar.

2. Choose Customize from the resulting shortcut menu.

3. Click a category in the scrolling list.

4. Click on the displayed buttons. Their functions will be described at the bottom of the dialog box.

5. If you see a button you like that isn't already on one of your toolbars, drag it to the toolbar of your choice and release the mouse button.

6. Kerplunk. You have a customized toolbar.

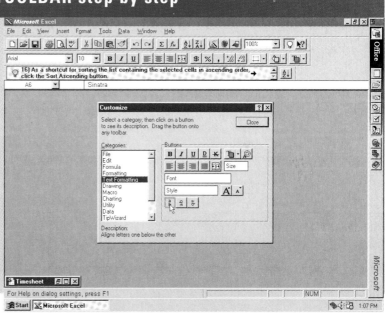

Need some button ideas to get you started? You might want to add a Find button to your standard toolbar if you are always looking for lost files. Or if you are constantly adding CellNotes, treat yourself to a text box button. If you frequently lock and unlock cells, add a Lock button. There's a Freeze and Unfreeze button that comes in handy, too. Hey, it's your computer.

# AUTOFILL

AutoFill watches you type and can automatically fill in linear date, time, and numeric progressions. For example, if you type **Jan** in one column and **Feb** in the next, you can ask Excel to AutoFill and it will continue with Mar, Apr, and so on. If, instead, you wanted to include columns for quarterly subtotals (and, so, labeled the first five columns "**January 1998**, **February 1998**, **March 1998, Q1, April 1998**"), Excel could fill in the rest of the year including the quarters (Q2, Q3, and Q4), creating a total of 16 columns ending with the two columns December 1998 and Q4.

And you needn't limit yourself to months and years. AutoFill works with just about any linear progression Excel can recognize. You could type **Store 1** and **Store 2** and have Excel provide Store 3 and so on. AutoFill works for numeric projections as well. If you type **10** in one cell and **20** in the next, AutoFill can provide 30, 40, and so forth. Time increments are possible. Typing **1:00** and **2:00** will cause Excel to fill with 3:00 and on and on.

Here are the general steps for AutoFilling:

1. Enter the first item in the first cell (**Jan-98**, for example).

| A1 | | jan-98 | |
|---|---|---|---|
| | **A** | **B** | **C** |
| **1** | jan-98 | | |
| **2** | | | |

2. Enter the next item (**Feb-98**, for example) in an adjacent cell either to the right of or below the first entry if you want the entries to increase, or in a cell to the left of or above the first entry for decreasing fills.
3. Select both cells, and point to the fill handle—a small square at the bottom-right corner of the cell pointer. (The mouse pointer changes to a black cross when you point to the right spot.)

| A1 | ▼ | 1/1/1998 |
| --- | --- | --- |
|   | **A** | **B** | **C** |
| **1** | Jan-98 | Feb-98 |   |
| **2** |   |   |   |

4. Drag the fill handle in the desired direction, stopping after highlighting the correct number of cells.
5. Release the mouse button to complete the series. (Notice how the year and month both increase in the thirteenth cell.)

| A1 | ▼ | 1/1/1998 |
| --- | --- | --- |

| | A | B | C | D | E | F | G | H | I | J | K | L | M | N |
| --- | --- | --- | --- | --- | --- | --- | --- | --- | --- | --- | --- | --- | --- | --- |
| **1** | Jan-98 | Feb-98 | Mar-98 | Apr-98 | May-98 | Jun-98 | Jul-98 | Aug-98 | Sep-98 | Oct-98 | Nov-98 | Dec-98 | Jan-99 | |
| **2** | | | | | | | | | | | | | | |

# Creating Custom Fill Lists

This is *very* cool. You can create custom fill lists and drop them in by simply typing the first item in the list and dragging the fill handle. The steps are involved, but worth it. Suppose you want a list of your branch offices in a particular order.

1. If the list is already typed on a worksheet, select it. (Maui, Kauai, and Molokai, let's say).

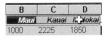

| B | C | D |
| --- | --- | --- |
| **Maui** | **Kauai** | **Molokai** |
| 1000 | 2225 | 1850 |

2. Pick Options in the Tools menu.
3. Click the Custom Lists tab in the resulting dialog box.

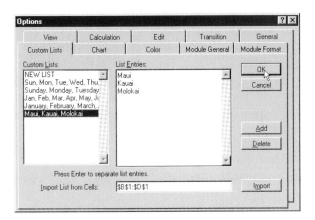

4. Click Import if you've selected the list back in step 1, or type the list in the List entries box if you have not selected the list items. separate items with commas or by pressing ENTER; do not use spaces.

5. Click OK.

6. To test, click in a blank cell and type the first entry.

7. Drag the fill handle and the list should appear. (I told you this is cool.)

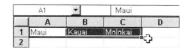

# KEYBOARD SHORTCUTS

There are many, many keyboard shortcuts available in Excel. I'll mention the ones I am addicted to throughout this book. But if you'd like to see, and perhaps print, a more or less comprehensive list, here's how to display it using Excel's online Help.

## DISPLAYING SHORTCUT KEYS step by step

1. Open Help and in the Index tab, type **keyboard.**

2. Click the Display button.

3. Double-click the topic Using shortcut keys.

4. Click the category of shortcut keys that interests you.

5. To print the shortcuts, use the Print Topic command reached with the Options button.

6. To see shortcuts for other categories of work, use the Back button and repeat steps 4 and 5.

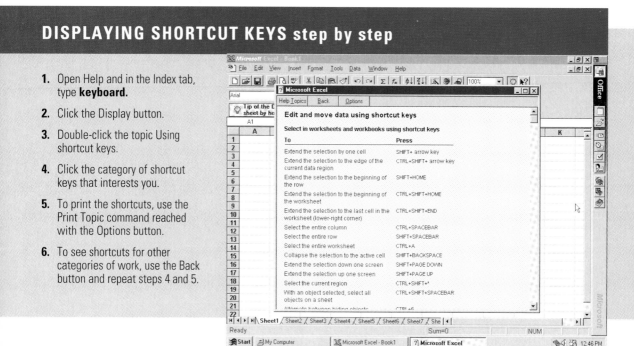

# WHAT NEXT?

Once you get that worksheet created, chances are very good that you'll need to rearrange it. That's the topic of Chapter 4.

CHAPTER

4

# Rearranging Worksheets

INCLUDES

- Moving, copying, deleting, and inserting cells

- Moving, copying, deleting, and inserting rows

- Moving, copying, deleting, and inserting columns

- Sorting data in worksheets

- Avoiding problems when rearranging formulas

# FAST FORWARD

## MOVE CELLS ➤ *pp 82-83*

1. Highlight the cells to be moved.
2. Point to the border of the selection (your mouse pointer will change to a white arrow when you are pointing properly).
3. Drag and drop them into their new location.
4. Check for unwanted changes in cell references.

## COPY CELLS ➤ *pp 83-84*

1. Either use the preceding steps while holding down the CTRL key, or select the cells to be copied.
2. Use the Edit menu's Copy command or CTRL-C. (This changes the contents of your Clipboard.)
3. Activate the first cell in the area where you plan to paste the copy.
4. Visually check to be sure the paste will not overwrite important cell data.
5. Press ENTER.
6. Check for proper formula functioning and referencing.

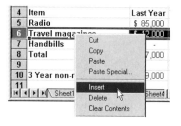

## SORT WORKSHEET ELEMENTS ➤ *pp 84-86*

1. Select a cell in the range you wish to sort.
2. Choose Sort from the Data menu.
3. Specify one or more rows or columns to be used as sort keys.
4. Specify ascending or descending sort order.
5. Click OK.

## INSERT ROWS ➤ *p 86*

1. Click the row below where you need to add new rows. (To insert multiple rows, select multiple rows.)
2. Choose Row from the Insert menu.
3. The row(s) will be inserted and other rows will be pushed down and renumbered.
4. Check for formula and referencing problems.

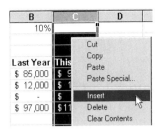

## INSERT COLUMNS ➤ *p 87*

1. Click to choose the column where you want to insert a new, blank column. (To insert multiple columns, select multiple columns.)
2. Choose Columns from the Insert menu.
3. The column(s) will be inserted and other columns will be pushed to the right and relettered.
4. Check for formula and referencing problems.

(The shortcut menu reached with the right mouse button also contains an Insert command.)

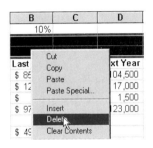

## DELETE WORKSHEET PARTS ➤ *pp 87-88*

1. Select the unwanted part(s).
2. Choose Delete from the Edit menu.
3. The deleted part(s) will disappear from the screen.
4. Check for formula and referencing problems.

(The shortcut menu reached with the right mouse button also contains a Delete command.)

## SPOT POTENTIAL PROBLEMS
## WITH AUDITING TOOLS ➤ *pp 93-94*

1. Select the cell(s) you wish to change.
2. Choose Auditing from the Tools menu.
3. Select Trace Dependents.
4. Arrows will radiate from the selected cell to dependent cells, showing which cells will be affected by changes to the original cell(s).

(You can also use the Auditing toolbar to help spot and fix problems. See Chapter 12 for details.)

*Clipboard: A chunk of your computer's memory where items are temporarily stored when you use the Cut and Copy commands. Every time you issue a Cut or Copy command the old contents of the Clipboard are replaced with the new material. Quitting Windows deletes the Clipboard contents.*

**I**nevitably, you'll wish you had designed your worksheet differently. You'll need to add or delete employees on a payroll worksheet or insert quarterly subtotal columns— you know the drill. Such changes will make it necessary for you to insert extra rows or columns, move things around, or squirt a few cells like watermelon seeds out of the universe.

# MOVING CELLS

| | Item | Last Year | This Year | Next Year |
|---|---|---|---|---|
| 4 | | | | |
| 5 | Radio | $ 85,000 | $ 95,000 | $ 104,500 |
| 6 | Travel magazines | $ 12,000 | $ 17,000 | $ 18,700 |
| 7 | Handbills | $ - | $ 1,500 | $ 1,650 |
| 8 | Total | $ 97,000 | $ 113,500 | $ 124,850 |
| 9 | | | | |
| 10 | 3 Year non-radio costs | $ 50,850 | | |
| 11 | | | | |

Moving the contents of a cell or cells and other items can be as simple as cutting and pasting:

1. Select the cell or cells.
2. Cut with the CTRL-X keyboard shortcut or choose Cut from the Edit menu.
3. The information moves to the Clipboard (obliterating whatever was there previously).
4. Click the top-leftmost cell to select it to receive the moved material.
5. Paste, either by pressing ENTER or CTRL-V, or using the Edit menu's Paste command.

Excel does not warn you if your pasting will overwrite the contents of a cell, so keep your eye on the screen. If you use Undo in time, you can undo any accidental overwrite.

You can also move cells, rows, and columns by selecting them and using drag-and-drop. Here are the general steps.

1. Highlight the cells you want to move.
2. Drag at their edges with the arrow-shaped pointer.

**CAUTION**

*When you move, insert, and delete cells, formulas are sometimes affected. Check your work carefully after rearranging worksheets!*

3. Release the mouse button to drop the selected items at the outlined position.

Unlike cut-and-paste, drag-and-drop *does* warn you if you are going to overwrite nonblank cells. Click OK to replace the previous cell contents with whatever you are dragging, or choose Cancel to abort the drag-and-drop.

# COPYING CELLS

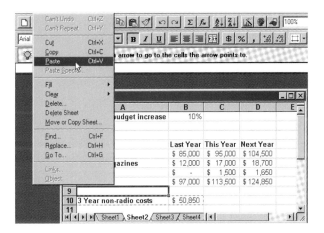

To copy cells:

1. Select the desired cells by dragging with your mouse or by clicking in the first cell and shift-clicking in the last cell of interest.

2. Copy with the CTRL-C keyboard shortcut or the Edit menu's Copy command. (Remember any existing Clipboard contents will be replaced by the data you copy.)

3. Select the upper-leftmost cell to receive the copy by clicking in it.

4. Either press ENTER to Paste once and stop the marching ants, or use the Paste command on the Edit menu to paste in more than one location.

You can also copy with drag-and-drop, as illustrated here.

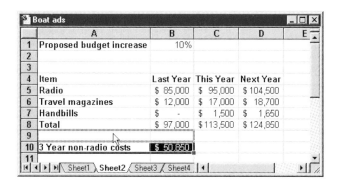

1. Select the cells of interest.

2. Hold down the CTRL key while dragging. The mouse pointer will have a small plus sign next to it.

3. When you release the mouse, the selected cells will be copied to the new location.

# SORTING CELL DATA

You can sort groups of cells in ascending or descending order, using up to three sort keys at once. Excel will even use headings in your worksheet to "name" the sort keys. For instance, if you had a spreadsheet containing client names, dates, and times, you could simultaneously sort on client (alphabetically), then date, and then time. Figure 4.1 illustrates how to set up a sort.

## The Importance of Careful Sorting

Although versions 5 and later of Excel can *usually* automatically detect and select the data you intend to sort (and only that data), sorting

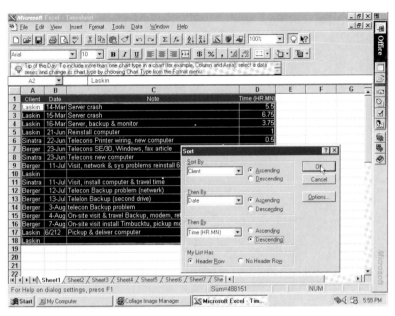

**Figure 4.1** Excel lets you sort using up to three keys at once

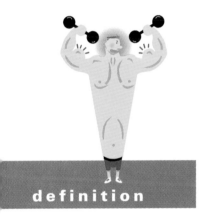

***Sort Keys:*** *Headings used by Excel when performing sorts. For example, if you have columns labeled Age, Last Name, and First Name, any one or all three of these column headings could be used as sort keys.*

in a spreadsheet is still risky business. You must be sure that you and Excel select everything you want to sort, and nothing else. For instance, in Figure 4.1, if you select all the clients' names, dates, and notes, but forget to select (or if you deselect) their time entries, the time entries will not move, but the names will, giving clients wrong times. You can use Undo to fix this, but you should save before you sort, so you can close a messed-up worksheet without saving, if necessary. Then you can reload the good, unsorted version (or make a copy and try your sort on *it* ). That said, here are the steps for sorting:

1. Select just the cells (or rows or columns) you want to sort. Include headings if you wish.
2. Choose Sort from the Data menu.
3. Click the Options button if you want to sort by columns instead of rows. (Excel sorts by rows unless you tell it otherwise.)
4. If you want to use headings as sort keys, pick that option in the dialog box.
5. Pick the first sorting key. If you use headings for keys, you'll see them listed in drop-down lists.

6. Next, tell Excel whether you want the sort to produce ascending or descending results. (In Figure 4.1 we wanted the clients alphabetized, and entries displayed in chronological order within client, so an ascending sort was specified for client and date. Descending was used for the time since we wanted the largest chunks of time listed first for each day.)

7. If you want to do additional sorts, move to the next key box and repeat the process. Do it again, if necessary, for a three-level sort.

8. When you've set up the sorting specifications, click OK and inspect the results.

| | A | B | C | D |
|---|---|---|---|---|
| 1 | Client | Date | Note | Time (HR.MN) |
| 2 | Laskin | 14-Mar | Server crash | 5.5 |
| 3 | Laskin | 15-Mar | Server crash | 6.75 |
| 4 | Laskin | 16-Mar | Server, backup & monitor | 3.75 |
| 5 | Laskin | 21-Jun | Reinstall computer | 1 |
| 6 | Sinatra | 22-Jun | Telecons Printer wiring, new computer | 0.5 |
| 7 | Berger | 23-Jun | Telecons SE/30, Windows, fax article | 0.75 |
| 8 | Sinatra | 23-Jun | Telecons new computer | 0.25 |
| 9 | Berger | 11-Jul | Visit, network & sys problems reinstall 6.0.8 on two machines | 3 |
| 10 | Laskin | | | |
| 11 | Sinatra | 11-Jul | Visit, install computer & travel time | 0.5 |
| 12 | Berger | 12-Jul | Telecon Backup problem (network) | 0.5 |
| 13 | Berger | 13-Jul | Telelon Backup (second drive) | 0.5 |
| 14 | Berger | 3-Aug | telecon Backup problem | 0.5 |
| 15 | Berger | 4-Aug | On-site visit & travel Backup, modem, reformat & reinstall | 4.25 |
| 16 | Berger | 7-Aug | On-site visit install Timbucktu, pickup modems | |
| 17 | Laskin | 6/212 | Pickup & deliver computer | 1.25 |

# INSERTING ROWS

It's easy to insert additional rows in a worksheet. One way is to select the entire row *below* the place where you want a new blank row. For example, click on the row number at the left edge of row number 4 to select row 4. Then choose the Rows command from the Insert menu. You will see a new, blank row 4, and the old contents of row 4 will become row 5. All of the rows that follow will also be pushed down and renumbered. Formulas will usually accommodate insertions like this, but, as always, check your work.

To insert multiple rows, *select* multiple rows before issuing the Insert command. For instance, to insert three rows in our earlier example, you could select rows 4, 5, and 6.

# INSERTING COLUMNS

To insert a column, click on the label of the column where you want the new column to appear. For instance, if you want a blank column at column B, select column B. Use the Columns command on the Insert menu, or click the right mouse button and choose Insert from the shortcut menu. You will see a new, blank column B, and the old contents of column B will become column C. All of the columns that follow will also be pushed right and relabeled. Formulas will usually allow for insertions like this, but check your work to be sure.

To insert multiple columns, select multiple columns before using the Insert command. That is, to insert three columns in our example, you could select columns B, C, and D.

# INSERTING CELLS

You can insert empty cells into an existing worksheet, thereby pushing existing cells either to the right of the insertion point or down from the insertion point. Highlight the area where you want to insert new blank cells and then use the Insert menu's Cells command (or click the right mouse button and choose Insert from the shortcut menu that appears). The Insert dialog box comes up, asking you if you want to shift cells right or down, or insert an entire row or entire column. This pushes cells as you might expect, although it can ruin the appearance of your worksheet. Use Undo if you are unhappy with the results.

# INSERTING AS YOU PASTE

Sometimes, instead of pasting over existing cells, you'll want to make room for new items as you paste them. If so, select the items to be pasted, then cut or copy them to the Clipboard. The Insert Cut Cells command will appear on the Edit menu. Activate the cell, row, or column where you want to insert the Clipboard contents, and choose the Insert Cut Cells command. Check the effect upon formulas and the overall worksheet appearance after pasting this way.

# DELETING PARTS OF A WORKSHEET

The Delete command on the Edit menu can be used to delete unwanted rows, columns, or cells. This closes up the space made by

the deletion. For example, if you select all of column B and use the Edit menu's Delete command, the contents of column C will shift left and become column B, D will become C, etc., almost to infinity (or the maximum width of the worksheet).

The same basic process occurs when you delete rows. Deleting row 4 moves row 5's contents up, making those cells the new row 4, and so on.

If you select an irregular collection of cells (something other than a complete row or column), Excel will ask how you want remaining cells to move when they fill in the newly emptied space.

Deletions of rows, columns, or cells can affect formulas, particularly if you remove cells that are referenced by formulas. Check your work.

# CLEARING PARTS OF A WORKSHEET

Clearing removes cell contents but does not move the contents of other cells to fill in the newly emptied space. Highlight the cell or cells you want to clear, then press the DEL key or use one of the Clear command choices on the Edit menu. You can clear every aspect of the cell or just selected features like formats, contents, or notes.

# HOW FORMULAS REACT TO WORKSHEET DESIGN CHANGES

I've alluded to a whole host of potential problems with formulas when modifying worksheet designs, but it's worth listing them here. Some changes can have a profound effect on formulas, others are benign. But whenever you fiddle with a cell that is referenced in a formula (even if the formula is in some other worksheet or file), there is the potential for trouble. This is particularly true when you:

- Insert rows, columns, or cells
- Delete rows, columns, or cells
- Move cells, rows, or columns referred to by formulas
- Clear cells referred to by formulas
- Change the data type of a cell (e.g., numbers to text)

Careful planning at the beginning of your projects, Excel's good nature, and its paternal instincts should minimize problems. But you need to anticipate the effects of changes, then test modified worksheets carefully. Let's take the issues one at a time using that small advertising budget exercise from previous chapters. I've turned on the View Formulas option to display the formulas in their cells, making it easier to see what's going on:

| | A | B | C | D |
|---|---|---|---|---|
| 1 | Proposed budget increase | 0.1 | | |
| 2 | | | | |
| 3 | | | | |
| 4 | Item | Last Year | This Year | Next Year |
| 5 | Radio | 85000 | 95000 | =(C5*$B$1)+C5 |
| 6 | Travel magazines | 12000 | 17000 | =(C6*$B$1)+C6 |
| 7 | Handbills | 0 | 1500 | =(C7*$B$1)+C7 |
| 8 | Total | =SUM(B5:B7) | =SUM(C5:C7) | =SUM(D5:D7) |
| 9 | | | | |
| 10 | 3 Year non-radio costs | =SUM(B6:D7) | | |
| 11 | | | | |

*Boat ads — Sheet1 \ Sheet2 \ Sheet3 \ Sheet4 \ Shee*

# Effects of Inserting Rows

Inserting rows and columns can be either very straightforward or fiendishly tricky. For instance, if you were to insert a row between Radio and Travel magazines (between rows 5 and 6), the SUM formulas in Row 9 that calculate *total* advertising costs will automatically change to include the newly inserted row.

| | A | B | C | D |
|---|---|---|---|---|
| 1 | Proposed budget increase | 0.1 | | |
| 2 | | | | |
| 3 | | | | |
| 4 | Item | Last Year | This Year | Next Year |
| 5 | Television | | | |
| 6 | Radio | 85000 | 95000 | =(C6*$B$1)+C6 |
| 7 | Travel magazines | 12000 | 17000 | =(C7*$B$1)+C7 |
| 8 | Handbills | 0 | 1500 | =(C8*$B$1)+C8 |
| 9 | Total | =SUM(B6:B8) | =SUM(C6:C8) | =SUM(D6:D8) |
| 10 | | | | |
| 11 | 3 Year non-radio costs | =SUM(B7:D8) | | |

*Boat ads — Sheet1 \ Sheet2 \ Sheet3 \ Sheet4 \ Shee*

This is probably, but *not always*, what you want. In this example, if you are adding a new expense line like *Television*, perhaps, you are okay, since the SUM formulas are computing *total costs*. But, suppose

*Use named ranges to minimize insertion problems. See Chapters 1 and 6 regarding named ranges.*

you inserted the new row because you plan to put some non-expense items in the new row, like the percent of change in the advertising costs. In that instance, you wouldn't want those newly inserted percentages to be included in your subtotals below, where they would erroneously increase the subtotals. And, there's another potential gotcha. Can you spot it?

The formula that finds three-year non-radio advertising costs (in what is now cell B11) does not automatically refer to the newly inserted cells after you insert the row! So, if you *do* put additional non-radio advertising costs in the newly inserted row, they will be ignored by the formula in B11, making for a too-small result. You need to modify the B11 formula.

Check out the formulas in D7 and D9. As we already discussed, D9's references have changed to automatically include the new row. The formula in D7 now refers to cell C7, properly reacting to the insertion. Because we used absolute addressing each time we specified cell B1, all the old formulas got that right too. Had we not used absolute addressing here, that might have been a problem, however. Check your work!

There is no formula in cell D6 and it needs one. It can be copied (or filled down) from D5, or copied or filled up from D7. Alternately, you can just type a new formula from scratch.

## Inserting at the Tops and Bottoms of Lists

Although inserting new rows in the middle of areas serviced by a range reference includes the new row in most formulas, inserting at the top or bottom does not. Here, watch:

| | A | B | C | D |
|---|---|---|---|---|
| | Boat ads | | | |
| 1 | Proposed budget increase | 0.1 | | |
| 2 | | | | |
| 3 | | | | |
| 4 | Item | Last Year | This Year | Next Year |
| 5 | Television | | | |
| 6 | Radio | 85000 | 95000 | =(C6*$B$1)+C6 |
| 7 | Travel magazines | 12000 | 17000 | =(C7*$B$1)+C7 |
| 8 | Handbills | 0 | 1500 | =(C8*$B$1)+C8 |
| 9 | Total | =SUM(B6:B8) | =SUM(C6:C8) | =SUM(D6:D8) |
| 10 | | | | |
| 11 | 3 Year non-radio costs | =SUM(B7:D8) | | |

Sheet1 \ **Sheet2** \ Sheet3 \ Sheet4 \ Shee

If you insert a new row directly above the Radio line (above the old row 5), Excel will not include it in things like the SUM formulas used to create totals. You can see this by examining the formulas in B9, C9, and D9. You'll have the same problem if you insert a row or rows between the SUM formula line and the old *last* row. You'll need to modify the references after inserting this way.

# Effects of Inserting Columns

Excel reacts about the same way when you insert columns as it does when you insert rows. Insertions in the middle of ranges are usually included in references to the range, those on the left and the right are not. Check your work carefully.

# Effects of Moving Rows, Columns, or Cells

Excel does a pretty good job of keeping track of things when you move rows, columns, or cells around on the same worksheet. For example, you just saw Excel adjust formulas when things got moved down during a row insertion. Even absolute addressing can be maintained when referenced cells are moved. Here, the contents of cell B1 were cut, then pasted into cell A2. Notice that the absolute address references in cells D5 through D7 were automatically modified, and are correct even after the move:

| Boat ads | | | |
|---|---|---|---|
| **A** | **B** | **C** | **D** |
| 1 Proposed budget increase | | | |
| 2 0.1 | | | |
| 3 | | | |
| 4 Item | Last Year | This Year | Next Year |
| 5 Radio | 85000 | 95000 | =(C5*$A$2)+C5 |
| 6 Travel magazines | 12000 | 17000 | =(C6*$A$2)+C6 |
| 7 Handbills | 0 | 1500 | =(C7*$A$2)+C7 |
| 8 Total | =SUM(B5:B7) | =SUM(C5:C7) | =SUM(D5:D7) |
| 9 | | | |
| 10 3 Year non-radio costs | =SUM(B6:D7) | | |
| 11 | | | |

Sheet1 **Sheet2** Sheet3 Sheet4 Shee

| Next Year |
|---|
| =(C6*#REF!)+C6 |
| =(C7*#REF!)+C7 |
| =(C8*#REF!)+C8 |
| =SUM(D6:D8) |

This will not work if you cut from one sheet and paste to another sheet in the same workbook, or to a different file, however. If you do move referenced items off of a worksheet, you'll often see the error message "#REF!" in cells referencing the "lost" item.

Notice the error message in each cell that depends upon the moved cell that was B2. I simply need to show Excel the way to the missing data. Here are the general steps:

1. Select a confused formula (D5, perhaps).
2. Select the REF error in the Formula bar (including the # and !):

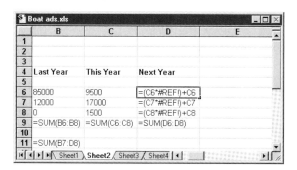

3. Either type the correct cell address (including sheet name, etc.), or click on the new cell location, which is often much easier than typing the whole address. In this example, I've switched to Sheet3 and clicked on cell A8 there.

4. Switch back to the original worksheet by clicking on the original worksheet tab and save the formula changes by clicking the Enter box or pressing ENTER.
5. Inspect the results from the new formula. If the problem is resolved, change other references as necessary. Don't forget, if an item was referred to absolutely before it was moved it will need to be referred to absolutely after the move!

Note that you may not need to correct each formula containing the #REF! error. This message will also appear in any cell affected by the results of another troubled cell.

# Effects of Deleting Rows, Columns, or Cells

The major problem with deletions is the obvious one. If you delete rows, columns, or cells that are referenced in formulas, the formulas may not work. Or worse yet, they may still work, but using different, incorrect data, thereby providing incorrect results.

# Effects of Data Type Changes

Formulas expect to see a specific type of data in cells. If you place text in a cell that is supposed to contain a number, for example, Excel will ignore the text when doing math and you will see #VALUE! in the cell(s) containing the formula. See Excel-specific books and online help for details.

# AUDITING TOOLS HELP SPOT POTENTIAL PROBLEMS

Before you insert, delete, or move things around, you can use several of Excel's auditing tools to help you see which cells are affected by each other. This can make it easier to understand what might happen if you redesign a worksheet. For example, by selecting the B1 cell in this example and choosing Tools|Auditing|Trace Dependents, arrows will radiate from the selected cell to dependent cells:

| | A | B | C | D | E |
|---|---|---|---|---|---|
| | Boat ads | | | | |
| 1 | Proposed budget increase | 10% | | | |
| 2 | | | | | |
| 3 | | | | | |
| 4 | Item | Last Year | This Year | Next Year | |
| 5 | Radio | $ 85,000 | $ 95,000 | $104,500 | |
| 6 | Travel magazines | $ 12,000 | $ 17,000 | $ 18,700 | |
| 7 | Handbills | $    - | $  1,500 | $  1,650 | |
| 8 | Total | $ 97,000 | $113,500 | $124,850 | |
| 9 | | | | | |
| 10 | 3 Year non-radio costs | $ 50,850 | | | |
| 11 | | | | | |

Sheet1 \ Sheet2 / Sheet3 / Sheet4 /

**habits &
strategies**

*Turn on the Auditing toolbar*

*to help spot and fix problems.*

*Check out Chapter 12 for*

*information about this and other*

*handy troubleshooting tools.*

To see how a cell gets its results, you can use the Precedents command to see the other cells involved in the conspiracy. Here, Excel is telling us that cells B6 through D7 are involved in the results being displayed in B10:

| | A | B | C | D | E |
|---|---|---|---|---|---|
| | B10 | =SUM(B6:D7) | | | |
| | **Boat ads** | | | | |
| 1 | Proposed budget increase | 10% | | | |
| 2 | | | | | |
| 3 | | | | | |
| 4 | Item | Last Year | This Year | Next Year | |
| 5 | Radio | $ 85,000 | $ 95,000 | $ 104,500 | |
| 6 | Travel magazines | $ 12,000 | $ 17,000 | $ 18,700 | |
| 7 | Handbills | $ - | $ 1,500 | $ 1,650 | |
| 8 | Total | $ 97,000 | $113,500 | $ 124,850 | |
| 9 | | | | | |
| 10 | 3 Year non-radio costs | $ 50,850 | | | |
| 11 | | | | | |

Sheet1 / Sheet2 / Sheet3 / Sheet4

You can use these commands repeatedly. The arrows will remain onscreen *and print on your printouts* until you choose Remove All Arrows from the Auditing submenu on the Tools menu. To learn more about auditing, read Chapter 12.

# CHAPTER 5

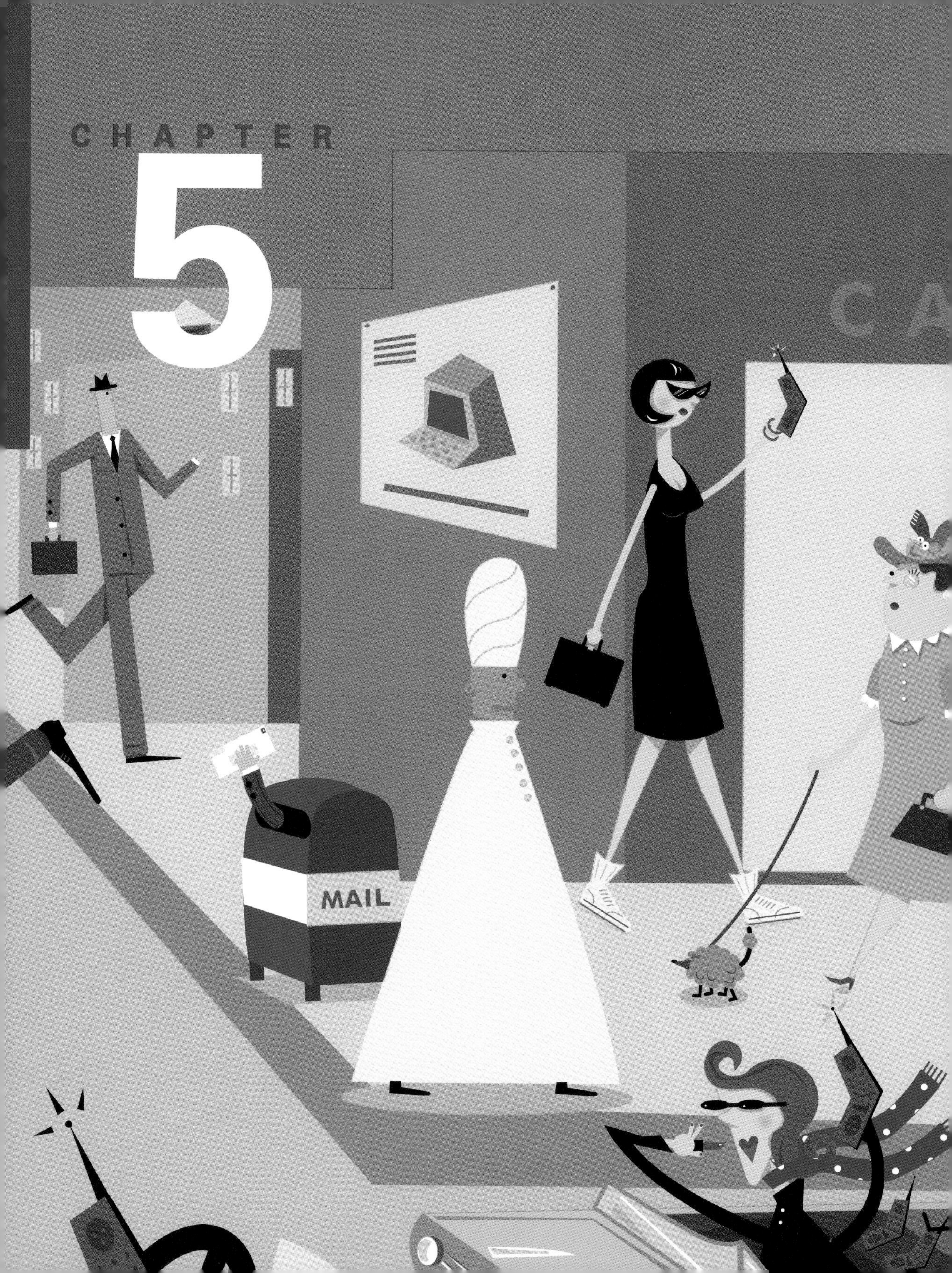

# Formatting Tricks

# FAST FORWARD

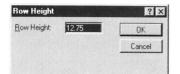

## CHANGE COLUMN WIDTHS ➤ *pp 101-102*

- To automatically adjust a column to fit its widest entry, double-click one of the lines separating the labels (letters).
- Or, you can select one or more columns and choose Format|Column|AutoFit.
- Alternatively, you can drag columns to new widths with the lines that separate column labels.
- To specify a column width in number of characters, select the column and right-click, then select the Column Width command. Enter the desired character count and click OK.

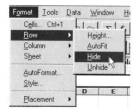

## CHANGE ROW HEIGHT ➤ *pp 102-103*

- Rows automatically adjust to fit their tallest entry.
- You can drag rows to new heights with the lines that separate row numbers.
- To specify a row height in points, select the row and right-click, then select the Row Height command. Enter the desired point size and click OK.

## HIDE AND REVEAL ROWS
## OR COLUMNS ➤ *pp 102-103*

1. Select the row(s) or column(s) to be hidden.
2. In the Format menu, choose Row and then Hide for rows, or Column and then Hide for columns.
3. The row(s) or column(s) will disappear and the row numbering or column letter labels will be noncontiguous.
4. To reveal, select the rows above and below the hidden rows or the columns to the right and left of hidden columns, then use the Unhide command on the Format Rows and Format Columns submenus.

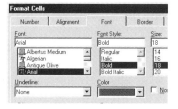

## AUTOMATICALLY
## APPLY FORMATTING ➤ *pp 103-104*

1. Select the cells you wish to format.
2. Choose AutoFormat from the Format menu.
3. Click on the various table format style names to preview the automatic format options in the dialog box.
4. Use the Options button to include or exclude formatting options.
5. Click OK.
6. Use Undo (CTRL-Z) if you dislike the results.

## ALTER THE APPEARANCE
## OF NUMBERS ➤ *pp 104-107*

1. Select the cell(s) containing the number(s) to be reformatted.
2. Either use the number format buttons on the Formatting toolbar, or right-click and choose Format Cells to use the Format Cells dialog box.

## CHANGE FONTS AND THEIR ATTRIBUTES ➤ *p 107*

1. Select cells or other objects containing text.
2. Use the formatting buttons (Bold, Italic, etc.) on the Formatting toolbar, or the Cells command on the Format menu. Visit the Fonts tab in the resulting Format Cells dialog box.

## CENTER TEXT ACROSS COLUMNS ➤ *pp 109-110*

1. Select the text to be centered, and the cells across which the text will be centered.
2. Use the Center Across Columns button on the Formatting toolbar or choose Cells in the Format menu and use the Center Across Selection option in the Alignment tab.

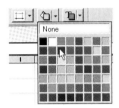

## ADD LINES AND BORDERS ➤ *pp 110-111*

1. Select the cells to be embellished.
2. Click the arrow on the Borders button on the Formatting toolbar to reveal a list of line and border choices.
3. Click the desired choice.
4. Click the Borders button again to add or change the appearance.

## CHANGE COLORS AND SHADING ➤ *p 111*

1. To change font colors (or gray shading on noncolor systems), select the cells containing text to be colorized.
2. Click the Font Color arrow on the Formatting toolbar.
3. Click the desired color from the resulting pallet.
4. To fill cells with a different color or gray shade, repeat steps 1-3 using the Color button on the Formatting toolbar instead.

## ADD OR REMOVE PAGE BREAKS ➤ *p 112*

To insert a page break:

1. Select the row beneath the desired page break point or the column to the left of the desired break point.
2. Choose Page Break from the Insert menu.

To remove a page break:

1. Select the row beneath the existing page break point or the column to the right of the break.
2. Choose Remove Page Break from the Insert menu. (This choice is only available when the appropriate row or column referred to in step 1 is properly selected.)

## COPY FORMATTING WITH FORMAT PAINTER ➤ *p 114*

1. Select the cell containing the format of interest.
2. Click the Format Painter button on the Standard toolbar.
3. "Marching ants" surround the selected cell, and the mouse pointer's shape changes.
4. Select the cell(s) to be formatted.
5. When you release the mouse button, the selected cells will be formatted.

(Pressing ESC cancels the Painter. Undo works after you've painted. If you double-click the Format Painter button, Painter stays active and you can paint multiple ranges. Click the button again to turn the Format Painter off.)

**C**hanging the appearance of a worksheet can make it easier to read and more professional looking. For example, Excel offers a number of automatic formatting features that color and shade row and column headings. These same formatting tools also highlight totals and subtotals, making them easier to see. The results can be quite striking.

On the other hand, too much formatting can waste valuable time and make you look like an amateur. The trick is to know when to quit. In this chapter, we'll look at some easy ways to make your work more presentable.

# CHANGING COLUMN WIDTHS AND ROW HEIGHTS

Row height automatically increases or decreases to match the largest font in the row. You can also manually change heights (to give a label some extra headroom, for example). But the more common task is to change column *widths* to accommodate wide text and numeric entries. Columns all start out at the same width and you can change them in a number of ways. If a text label is too wide for a column, one of two things happens. If the cell to the right of the too-long text is empty, the text "spills over" into the adjacent cell(s). If the neighboring cells are not empty, the text is truncated. (The text is still there, you just can't see it all.) One easy way to solve this problem is to make the cell containing the text wider. When cells containing numbers are too narrow, the numbers are frequently replaced with pound signs (####). Since these two problems occur regularly, let's start by looking at a few ways to widen columns.

## Using AutoFit to Automatically Adjust Columns

As I said earlier, columns all start out at a default width. Obviously, when you type long labels or numbers or when a formula creates large

**SHORTCUT**

*If you select multiple columns or rows before adjusting them, they will all change to the same dimensions.*

numbers, column widths might need to be adjusted. This is also true if you change font sizes, or add or remove text embellishments (like boldface, for example). Number formatting can necessitate column width changes too—when adding or expunging commas, for instance.

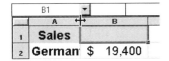

The easy way to change column widths is to double-click the line at the *right* of any column label that separates it from its neighbor. For example, in this illustration, clicking between column labels A and B will change the width of column A. Clicking at the line separating B and C would change B, and so on. Notice how the pointer's shape changes when you are in the right spot on the column label.

## Dragging to Change Row and Column Sizes

To change a column width by dragging, simply point to one of the edges in a column label and drag the column to a new width. Release the mouse button when the column width suits you.

Change a row's height by dragging the top of a row label. Release the mouse button when the height suits you.

## Row Height and Column Width Submenu Commands

There are menu commands that let you specify exact row height and column width settings. They are the submenus Row Height and Column Width, found under the Format menu.

Row height is expressed in *points*. The maximum height is 409.5 points. Why, I do not know. An entry of zero (0) hides the row, so be careful. If you do hide a row this way you will need to select the rows above and below, then specify a row height greater than zero to reveal

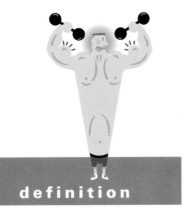

**definition**

***Points:** In typesetting and Excel, 1/72 of an inch. In the movie industry—with any luck, money enough for that new Mercedes.*

the row again. Incidentally, the default height in most worksheets is 12.75 points, which is a good thing to know if you accidentally change a row's height and want it to conform to the others.

Column widths are expressed as the number of *characters* (from 0 to 255) that can be displayed in a column. If the cell is too narrow to include a complete character you might see a fractional character width indicated. The worksheet's default font is used as the standard of measure. Here too, a value of zero hides the column's contents. If you hide a column this way, you will need to select the columns straddling the hidden one, then specify a column width greater than zero.

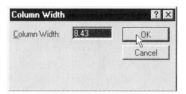

# AUTOFORMAT

AutoFormat lets you quickly change the color, typestyles, and overall appearance of your worksheets. Excel comes with a variety of predefined formats, each designed to make your work easier to read and more professional in appearance. You can apply them to an entire worksheet or just to selected areas. It's a good idea to test-print these formats in your spare time (yeah, right), before you start working on a big project with a tight deadline, since a few of the standard gray shades and colors might reproduce poorly on some printers. Here's how to use AutoFormat:

1. Select the cells you wish to format.
2. Choose AutoFormat from the Format menu.
3. Click the Options button if you wish to restrict the types of things changed by AutoFormat (typestyles, borders, etc.).
4. Scroll through the list of available formats, clicking on the ones of interest.
5. Preview the formats in the dialog box.
6. When you find one you like, click OK.

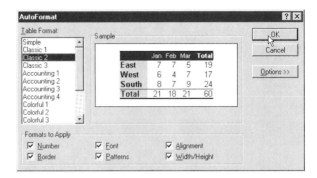

7. Excel will reformat the selected area(s) of your worksheet. This will often entail changes to column widths, fonts, border settings, and more.

8. If you hate what you see when AutoFormat (or should that be "Mr. Format"?) finishes, either use Undo or select the formatted cells, then revisit the AutoFormat dialog box and pick None (located at the bottom of the scrolling list).

# MANUAL FORMATTING

As you might suspect, anything AutoFormat can do, *you* can do. It is easy to fiddle with typestyles, colors, and all of that; just use the Formatting toolbar and a little restraint. The remainder of this chapter looks at manual formatting techniques.

**upgrade note**

*Excel 7 offers many improvements in number formatting! For example, it is much easier to specify formats for everyday things like phone numbers without resorting to creating custom formatting codes.*

# ALTERING A NUMBER'S APPEARANCE

By now you know that you can change a number's appearance when you enter it by simply including the desired commas, decimal

*If you forget the purpose of a button, remember that you can momentarily hover the mouse pointer over the button to read its name.*

points, currency symbols, etc. Or you can go back later and apply these number formats to cells. Some of the formatting options have their own buttons on the toolbars, as shown here:

Add dollar formatting

Add commas

Decrease decimal

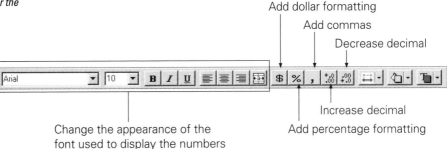

Increase decimal

Change the appearance of the font used to display the numbers

Add percentage formatting

## Quick Number Formatting

Excel knows how to format phone numbers, currency, ZIP codes, and much more. To use this built-in wisdom, simply select the cell(s) to be formatted and right-click, then select Format Cells. You'll see a dialog box like this one:

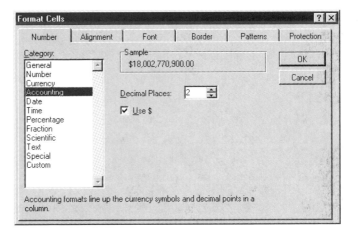

Click the Number tab if necessary to bring it to the forefront, then click a format type listed at the left side of the box and read the description. Unless the active cell is empty, you'll even see a sample

of the formatting applied to the first of your selected cells in the Sample portion of the dialog box. The Special choice reveals a whole list of handy formats:

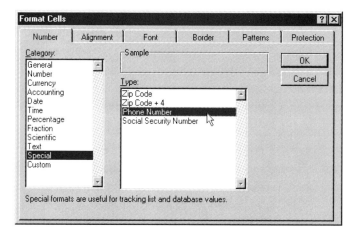

You can make your own special formats for things like part numbers. This requires at least a cursory understanding of *format codes*, the next topic (which you are encouraged to skip, busy person).

*If the number has more digits to the right of the decimal than there are placeholders in the format, the number gets rounded. If the number has more digits to the left of the decimal point than there are placeholders, the extra digits are displayed.*

## Applying Format Codes

Format codes let you design specific (heretofore undreamed of) number formatting schemes.

The process involves creating *placeholders* (#) for numbers. You do this by including the following format codes in a section.

| To display | Type this |
|---|---|
| 1234.59 as 1234.6 | ####.# |
| 8.9 as 8.900 | #.000 |
| 12 as 12.0 and 1234.568 as 1234.57 | #.0# |
| 5.25 as 5 1/4 and 5.3 as 5 3/10, with aligned division symbols | #???/??? |
| .5 as 0.5 | 0.## |

To display a comma as a thousands separator or to scale a number by a multiple of a thousand, include a comma in the number format, as follows.

| To display | Use this format code |
| --- | --- |
| 12000 as 12,000 | #,### |
| 12000 as 12 | #, |
| 12200000 as 12.2 | 0.0,, |

See the blue box on the following page to find out how to create and save your very own Format Codes.

# CHANGING FONT SIZES AND ATTRIBUTES

To change the size of a font in a cell, select the cell or cells to be victimized, and use the drop-down Font Size list found on the Formatting toolbar. Alternatively, you can make a more laborious visit to the Format Cells dialog box as described previously, this time using the Font tab.

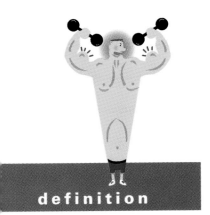

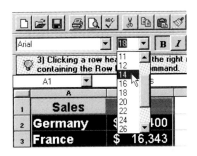

*Justified:* *In typesetting, the process of forcing right and left margins to be perfectly straight, even when it makes inter-word and inter-character spacing look ridiculous. This fad, which peaked once in the '70s, is becoming stylish yet again.*

# ADJUSTING TEXT ALIGNMENT

Cell text can be centered, right-aligned, left-aligned, justified, and even (forgive us, Gutenberg) stood on-end. Here's the short course:

By default, numbers are right-aligned and text is left-aligned. They need not stay that way. The obvious cravings to change things can be

## CUSTOMIZING FORMAT CODES step by step

1. Select a cell or cells.

2. Right-click to bring up the shortcut menu.

3. Choose Format Cells.

4. Click the Number tab if necessary to bring it forward.

5. Choose Custom from the list.

6. Click to pick a format from the list to use as a starting point.

7. Modify the format, watching the sample change as you work. (You can include fixed numbers, letters, and punctuation, if necessary.)

satisfied by selecting cells and clicking the appropriate Formatting toolbar buttons (Align Left, Center, or Align Right), shown in the next illustration. (Hover the mouse pointer over a button whenever its function is not obvious to you.)

To get *really* classy, you're gonna have to visit the Format Cells dialog box and then select the Alignment tab. It is *here* that you can commit untold crimes against good taste.

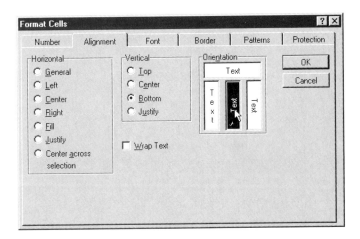

# WRAPPING TEXT IN CELLS

Remember how text disappears in a cell when the cell's too narrow and its neighbor is not empty? Instead of changing the entire column's width to accommodate the long label, you can cause the text to wrap in cells, thereby increasing the row height but leaving the column width unchanged. Here's how. Select the cell or cells you wish to make tall and narrow, then visit the Alignment tab in the Format Cells dialog box and click to place an x in the Wrap Text box. Words will wrap from one line to the next, increasing the row height as necessary. For example, here the text in cells A4 and A5 have been wrapped. Notice the increased row height in these two rows:

| | A | B | C | D |
|---|---|---|---|---|
| 1 | **Proposed Ticket Price changes** | | | |
| 2 | | Current | Proposed | **Difference** |
| 3 | Cruise | $ 9.95 | $ 12.95 | $ 3.00 |
| 4 | **Dinner** **Cruise** | $ 27.95 | $ 32.50 | $ 4.55 |
| 5 | **Blues** **Cruise** | $ 18.99 | $ 20.99 | $ 2.00 |

# CENTERING TEXT ACROSS COLUMNS

Sometimes it's nice to have a label float over more than one column. It's almost too easy.

1. Select the cell containing the word or words and the cells over which you want the text centered.

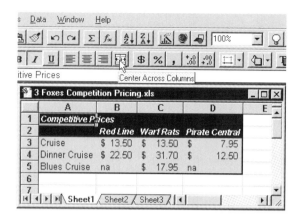

2. Click the Center Across Columns button. Pow.

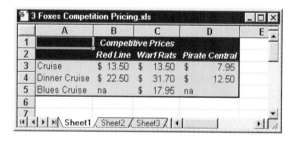

**Borders:** *Lines surrounding cells or groups of cells giving a "form-like" appearance to your worksheet.*

# USING BORDER BUTTONS AND COMMANDS

Quick borders can be created by *first selecting cells* and then using the Borders button on the Formatting toolbar:

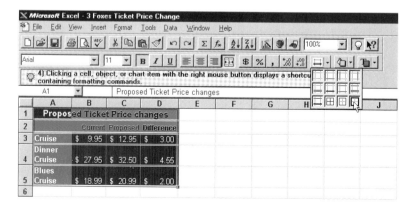

But to really wow the department heads, you'll need to visit the Border tab in the Format Cells dialog box. Here, you can play with all manner of decoration:

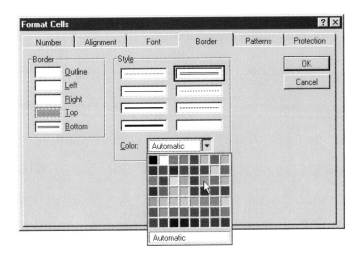

# CHANGING COLORS AND SHADING

If your computers (and output devices) are color-capable, you can add interest and emphasis to your masterpiece with the Color and Font Color buttons, both located on the Formatting toolbar. As usual, remember to select your prey first:

*When you pick a color or border from a drop-down palette, that new choice becomes the default; to apply it again, simply click the button. There is no need to revisit the palette until you want a different color or border or whatever.*

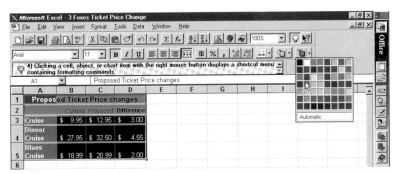

# INSERTING AND REMOVING PAGE BREAKS

Excel decides where to break pages when printing based on the Page Setup specifications you've made. You can force early page breaks (force Excel to start a new page before filling the previous one) by inserting your own page breaks:

- To force a break, select the row *beneath* the desired page break point. Choose Page Break from the Insert menu.
- To remove a forced break, select the row *below* the existing page break point, then choose Remove Page Break from the Insert menu. (This choice is only available when the appropriate row is selected.)

# USING STYLES

Styles are named collections of cell formatting decisions, including your choice of font, alignment, borders, patterns (shading), protection, and so on. Once you create and name styles, it is easy to apply them to other cells in your project. This can save a lot of manual formatting. Excel comes with a few predefined styles, and you can create your own. Let's take a look.

## Applying Styles

Excel's built-in styles can be applied by selecting the cell or cells to be embellished and selecting the Styles command on the Format menu:

*If you use a lot of custom styles, add the drop-down styles list to one of your toolbars.*

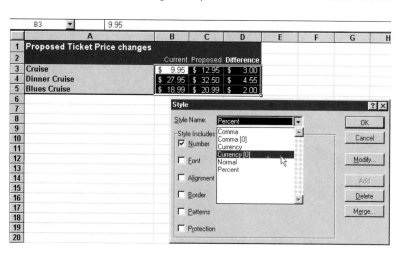

Once there, you simply pick a style from the drop-down menu to apply it. Since most of the predefined style tricks can be accomplished more quickly with toolbar buttons, the above steps are—how shall I say this?—*counter-productive*. Unless, of course, you have a need for your own very special styles. If that's the case, see the following blue box and learn how to create them. Otherwise, leapfrog to the section, "Using the Format Painter for Speedy Format Copying."

## CREATING STYLES step by step

1. Begin by formatting a cell the way you like it.

2. Choose Styles from the Formatting menu.

3. Type a new style name. The words "By Example" appear and the Add button un-dims.

4. Clear check boxes for any items you don't want included in the style and click Add.

5. Click OK. The style should now be available in the Style list.

6. Save the worksheet if you want to use the style in the future.

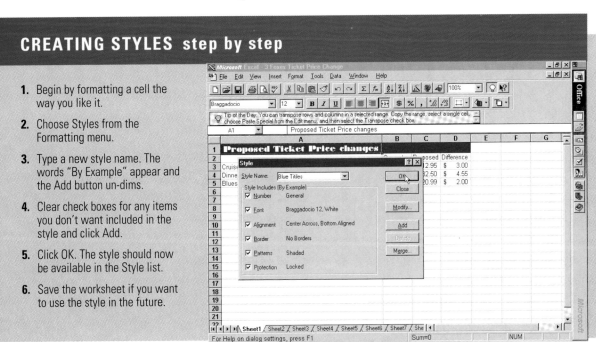

## Copying Styles to and from Other Workbooks

You can copy styles from one workbook to another. Here's how:

1. Open the workbook containing the styles of interest and the destination workbook.

2. Switch to the destination workbook (using the Windows menu), then click Style on the Format menu.

3. Choose Merge.

4. Select the name of the workbook that contains the styles you want to copy.

If the active workbook contains any styles that have the same name as styles you are copying, Excel asks if you want to merge the styles that have the same names. To replace styles, click Yes. To keep the existing styles, click No.

# USING THE FORMAT PAINTER FOR SPEEDY FORMAT COPYING

The format painter "looks" at the current cell's formatting and lets you "spread the formatting around" to other cells. Select a cell and click the Format Painter button to begin the process. Marching ants surround the cell and the pointer gets a cute little paintbrush.

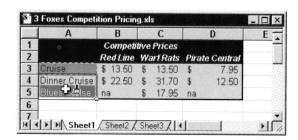

Drag to select the area to receive the formatting. That should do it.

# REMOVING FORMATTING

The process of unformatting cells can be pretty laborious unless you know this little trick:

1. Select the cells to be neutered.
2. Choose Style from the Format menu.
3. Select Normal.

Another way to go is to first select the cells, then choose Edit|Clear|Formats.

**SHORTCUT**

*When you double-click on the Format Painter button, it stays active and you can use it to paint multiple areas. Click it a third time to turn it off.*

# Organizing Large Projects

- Using named cell ranges

- Keeping headings in view

- Working with multisheet workbooks

- Naming worksheets

# FAST FORWARD

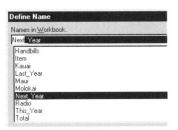

## HAVE EXCEL CREATE NAMED RANGES ➤ *p 121*

1. Select the cells to be named (include row and column labels in your selection).
2. Choose Name from the Insert menu.
3. Choose Create from the submenu.
4. Specify Top Row and Left Column if you've selected row and column labels.
5. Click OK.
6. Excel will find ranges, define and name them.

## NAME RANGES MANUALLY ➤ *pp 122-123*

1. Select the cell(s) of interest.
2. Choose Name from the Insert menu.
3. Pick Define from the submenu.
4. Check the Refers to box and change the reference, if necessary.
5. Examine the range name Excel proposes and change it if you wish.
6. Click OK to define the name. Range names are saved next time you save the worksheet.

## SEE A LIST OF NAMED RANGES ➤ *pp 123-124*

1. Choose Name from the Insert menu.
2. Choose Define from the submenu.
3. Read from the scrolling list of names. Selecting a name displays the associated cell range.

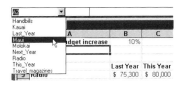

## REFER TO RANGES IN FORMULAS ➤ *p 124*

1. Begin the formula as usual.
2. At the point where you wish to insert a name, press F3, or use the drop-down list at the left end of the Formatting toolbar.
3. Pick the name from the resulting list.

## FREEZE TITLES ➤ *pp 125-126*

1. Select the row below the one you wish to freeze on the screen or the column to the right of the column you wish to freeze. To freeze both rows and columns, select the intersecting cell.
2. Choose Freeze Panes from the Window menu.
3. When you scroll, the frozen items will not scroll off of the screen.

## NAME WORKSHEETS ➤ *p 126*

To rename a worksheet, double-click on its tab and edit, or replace the tab's name in the resulting dialog box.

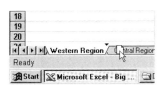

## MOVE WORKSHEETS ➤ *pp 126-127*

- To move a sheet within the same workbook, drag it to a new position.
- Either tile both workbooks on your screen and drag worksheets from one book to the other, or use the Edit menu's Move or Copy Sheet command to move sheets from one open workbook to another.

## COPY WORKSHEETS ➤ *pp 127-128*

1. Hold down CTRL and point to the tab for the sheet you wish to copy.
2. Drag your mouse to the tab position in the workbook where you want to place the copy. (The mouse pointer will change to include a page icon with a plus sign.)
3. Release the mouse button and the copy will be created and inserted.
4. Rename the new sheet if you like.

**O**ften, "bigger" is the reward for success—bigger boats, bigger houses, bigger headaches, bigger waistlines, bigger worksheets. All of these things can get more troublesome as they grow. And, while Excel can't help with your waistline, it does have features that can make large, complex spreadsheet projects more bearable. In this chapter we'll learn how to exploit those features.

# USING NAMES

It is easy to select groups of cells and give them meaningful names. (I hinted at this earlier.) There are many advantages to naming groups of cells, as you more easily can see by looking at a specific example. Take the worksheet in Figure 6.1, for instance.

I know, I know, this is a chapter about *big* projects and that's a *small* worksheet. But, hey. It's a small book, so we'll explore the concepts on a manageable scale and you can extrapolate on your own time.

Suppose you wanted to refer to the dollars relating to Radio expenses in Figure 6.1. They are contained in cells B5, C5, and D5. With very little effort you could name this range of three cells "Radio." You could then name the range of cells B6 through D6 "Travel," and so on. Another possibility would be to name *all* of the cells containing advertising expenditures (B5:D7) "Advertising" or something like that. And, perhaps cells B6:D7 could be called "NonRadio." Then, when you

*Name ranges and it will be easier to find and use them. Simply assign names to significant cell ranges, and then choose their names from the drop-down list at the left edge of the Formatting toolbar. You will "go to" the named range.*

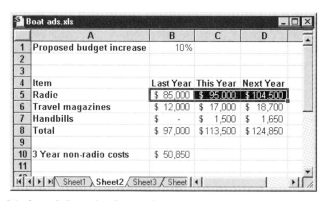

| | A | B | C | D |
|---|---|---|---|---|
| 1 | Proposed budget increase | 10% | | |
| 2 | | | | |
| 3 | | | | |
| 4 | Item | Last Year | This Year | Next Year |
| 5 | Radio | $ 85,000 | $ 95,000 | $ 104,500 |
| 6 | Travel magazines | $ 12,000 | $ 17,000 | $ 18,700 |
| 7 | Handbills | $    - | $  1,500 | $  1,650 |
| 8 | Total | $ 97,000 | $113,500 | $ 124,850 |
| 9 | | | | |
| 10 | 3 Year non-radio costs | $ 50,850 | | |
| 11 | | | | |

Boat ads.xls

Sheet1 Sheet2 Sheet3 Sheet

**Figure 6.1** A worksheet ripe for naming

created an equation in cell B10 to compute the non-radio advertising costs, you could use the formula =sum(advertising)-sum(radio) instead of =sum(B5:D7)-sum(B5:D5). Thereafter you could use the name "Non-Radio" when referring to the results of the equation in cell B10. Got the idea? Naming makes it easier to audit, troubleshoot, and understand worksheets too.

There are two ways to name things. You can ask Excel to create a name, or do it yourself. Whichever way you go, you can change the resulting name entries. Let's start with a look at automatic naming.

# Asking Excel to Create Names

If you select a range of cells containing labels, Excel can look for logical combinations of cells in those rows and columns, then name the useful ranges. For example, let's select the cells A4:D7, and ask Excel to name the various combinations.

| A4 ▼ | | Item | | |
|---|---|---|---|---|
| | **A** | **B** | **C** | **D** |
| **1** | Proposed budget i | 10% | | |
| **2** | | | | |
| **3** | | | | |
| **4** | Item | Last Year | This Year | Next Year |
| **5** | Radio | $ 85,000 | $ 95,000 | $ 104,500 |
| **6** | Travel magazines | $ 12,000 | $ 17,000 | $ 18,700 |
| **7** | Handbills | $ - | $ 1,500 | $ 1,650 |
| **8** | Total | $ 97,000 | $ 113,500 | $ 124,850 |
| **9** | | | | |
| **10** | 3 Year non-radio c | $ 50,850 | | |

1. Select a range of cells (A4 through D7 in this example).
2. Choose Name from the Insert menu.
3. Choose Create from the resulting submenu.
4. When you see the Create Names dialog box, specify Top Row and Left Column only, then click OK.

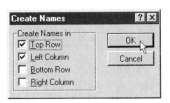

5. Excel creates named groups of cells without so much as a burp of acknowledgment. Which brings us to our next topic.

# Seeing Named Items

Once names have been defined you can see them by—nope, *not* by using the View menu, that would be too easy. You can see named ranges by dropping down the list at the left end of the Formatting toolbar. Or, you can choose Insert|Name|Define to see a dialog box like this one:

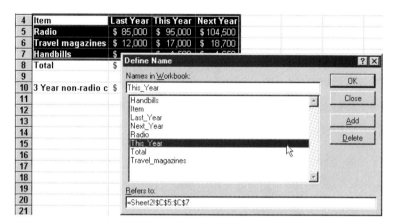

It contains a scrolling list of range names Excel made up all by itself. Selecting a name in the list displays the cell addresses to which the name refers (shown at the bottom of the dialog box). For example, the range named This_Year is on Sheet 2, cells $C$5:$C$7. Notice also how Excel has used the row and column labels to create the range names. And isn't that interesting how there are underscore characters rather than spaces between words in each name? That's because spaces are not permitted in range names. If you specify spaces, Excel will change them to underscore characters.

# Defining Names Yourself

Suppose you wanted to name the equation in cell B10 that computes the Non-Radio advertising costs so that you could use the name in your formulas. To name something:

1. Select the cell or cells of interest (B10, let's say).
2. Choose Name from the Insert menu.
3. Pick Define.
4. Check the Refers to box to ensure that the right cell reference appears there. (Change it if necessary.)

5. Consider the name Excel is proposing. Change it to something easier if you like (type or edit in the Names in Workbook portion of the dialog box).

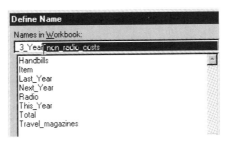

6. Click OK to define the name.
7. Save to make the name a permanent part of the workbook file.

# Listing All Named Items

It's often nice to know the names and ranges of all named items in your workbook. You can browse in the Define Name dialog box, as described earlier. But it is often quicker to get a complete list of all of the names in a worksheet, using a fairly convoluted process. Here are the steps.

1. Make sure you are finished naming everything in your workbook.
2. Select the cell where you want the top-leftmost entry of your list to appear. (I usually switch to a blank worksheet to do this.)
3. Choose Name from the Insert menu.
4. Choose Paste from the resulting submenu.
5. When you see the Paste Name dialog box, click the Paste List button.

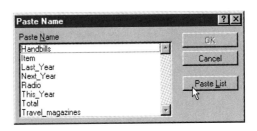

6. Excel will paste a list of all named items and their address references into the worksheet starting with the cell you selected in step 2.

| | A1 ▼ | | Handbills |
|---|---|---|---|
| | **A** | | **B** |
| **1** | Handbills | | =Sheet2!$B$7:$D$7 |
| **2** | Item | | =Sheet2!$B$5:$D$7 |
| **3** | Last_Year | | =Sheet2!$B$5:$B$7 |
| **4** | Next_Year | | =Sheet2!$D$5:$D$7 |
| **5** | Radio | | =Sheet2!$B$5:$D$5 |
| **6** | This_Year | | =Sheet2!$C$5:$C$7 |
| **7** | Total | | =Sheet2!$B$8:$D$8 |
| **8** | Travel_magazines | | =Sheet2!$B$6:$D$6 |
| **9** | | | |

# Referring to Ranges by Name

Once you've set up named items you can refer to them in formulas quite easily. Simply begin your equation normally, use the drop-down list at the left edge of the Formatting toolbar to bring up a list of names, and click the desired name in the list to insert it into your equation.

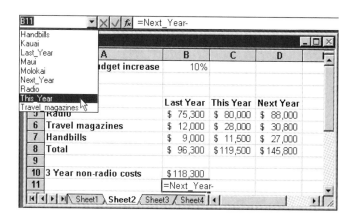

# Changing and Deleting Definitions

You can change or delete named items by visiting the Define Name dialog box, but use extreme caution when doing this. If you have a number of formulas that reference a name and you delete the name or change the cells to which the name refers, the formulas will not work properly. Check your work thoroughly after making name changes!

# FREEZING TITLES

When confronted with long or wide worksheets, it is often annoying to scroll. Almost immediately the row and/or column labels disappear. I don't know about you, but I can almost never remember the purpose of each row and column, so I continually scroll back and forth.

The trick to viewing big worksheets, of course, is to freeze titles. This technique make it much easier to work on big sheets. Take a look at Figure 6.2.

As soon as we scroll vertically, those column titles in Figure 6.2 are going to become invisible. And a scroll to the right is going to hide the client names located in column A. To freeze title rows and/or columns, you use the Freeze Panes command located on the Window menu. Once you freeze titles or columns or whatever, they do not scroll with the rest of the gang. You tell Excel where you want the freezing to begin by selecting the row *below* the row(s) you want to remain onscreen. To freeze a column, you select the column *to the right* of the column(s) you want to always keep onscreen. So, for example, to keep

**definition**

**Freezing:** *Fixing rows and/or columns so that when you scroll the frozen items stay put.*

**habits & strategies**

*When creating templates, set up features like frozen titles so that they will always be available when you start a new project.*

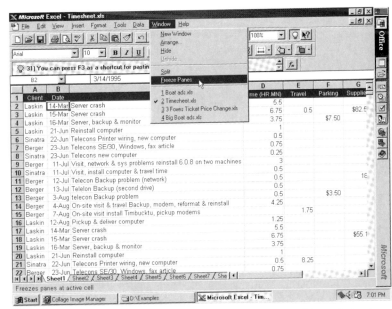

**Figure 6.2** Freezing can make it easier to cruise long and wide worksheets while keeping their labels in view

the column headings (Client, Date, Note, etc.) onscreen, and to keep the Client column (A) onscreen, you would select cell B2, then choose Window|Freeze Panes. To remove freezing (to thaw?), choose Unfreeze Panes in the Window menu.

# WORKING WITH MULTIPLE WORKSHEETS

As you have no doubt noticed, when you start a new project, Excel opens a workbook containing 16 worksheets. You can add additional worksheets if you like, and obviously there is no requirement that you use all 16 sheets for a given project. You can name individual worksheets, change their location in the workbook, summarize information contained on multiple sheets, and more. Let's take a look.

## Naming Worksheets

Each worksheet has a name. By default they are initially named Sheet1 through Sheet16. Their names appear on the tabs used to bring the sheets to the forefront. To rename a tab, simply double-click the worksheet's tab and then type the new name in the resulting dialog box.

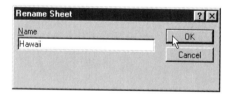

The tab will display the new name after you click OK to dismiss the dialog box.

# COPYING AND MOVING WORKSHEETS

You can copy or move worksheets within the same workbook or between workbooks. The simplest case is moving a worksheet from one location to another in the same workbook.

# Moving Worksheets Within a Workbook

To rearrange the order of tabs in a workbook, drag a tab to the desired new location. The mouse pointer changes and a small triangle appears to help you see where the tab will land when you release the mouse button.

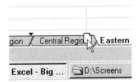

Here's how to make a copy of a sheet in the same workbook.

## COPYING A SHEET WITHIN A WORKBOOK  step by step

1. Click on the sheet's tab.

2. Hold down the CTRL key and drag. (Your mouse pointer will change to include a page and plus sign.)

3. When you reach the desired location for the copy, release the mouse button.

4. Excel will place a copy of the sheet at the desired location.

5. Rename the copied sheet if you like.

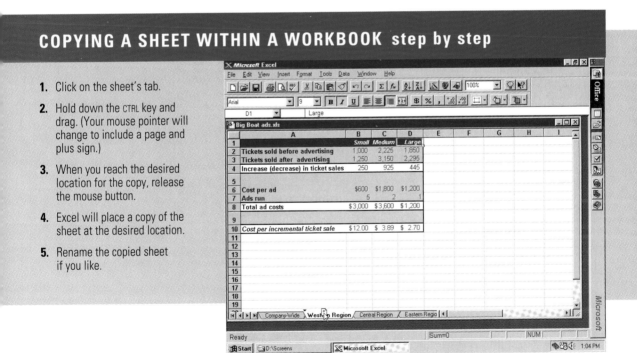

*If you are comfortable with tiling multiple windows, and if you have a big enough display area, you can display both workbooks on your screen at once and CTRL-drag from one workbook to the other to copy them or just plain drag to move them.*

# Copying Sheets to a Different Workbook

To copy a sheet from one workbook to another, open both workbooks, and before clicking OK in step 5 of the preceding section, choose the name of the second workbook in the To Book portion of the Move or Copy dialog box.

# Moving Sheets to a Different Workbook

To move sheets from one workbook to another, tile multiple workbooks on your screen and drag from one workbook to the other.

# CHAPTER 7

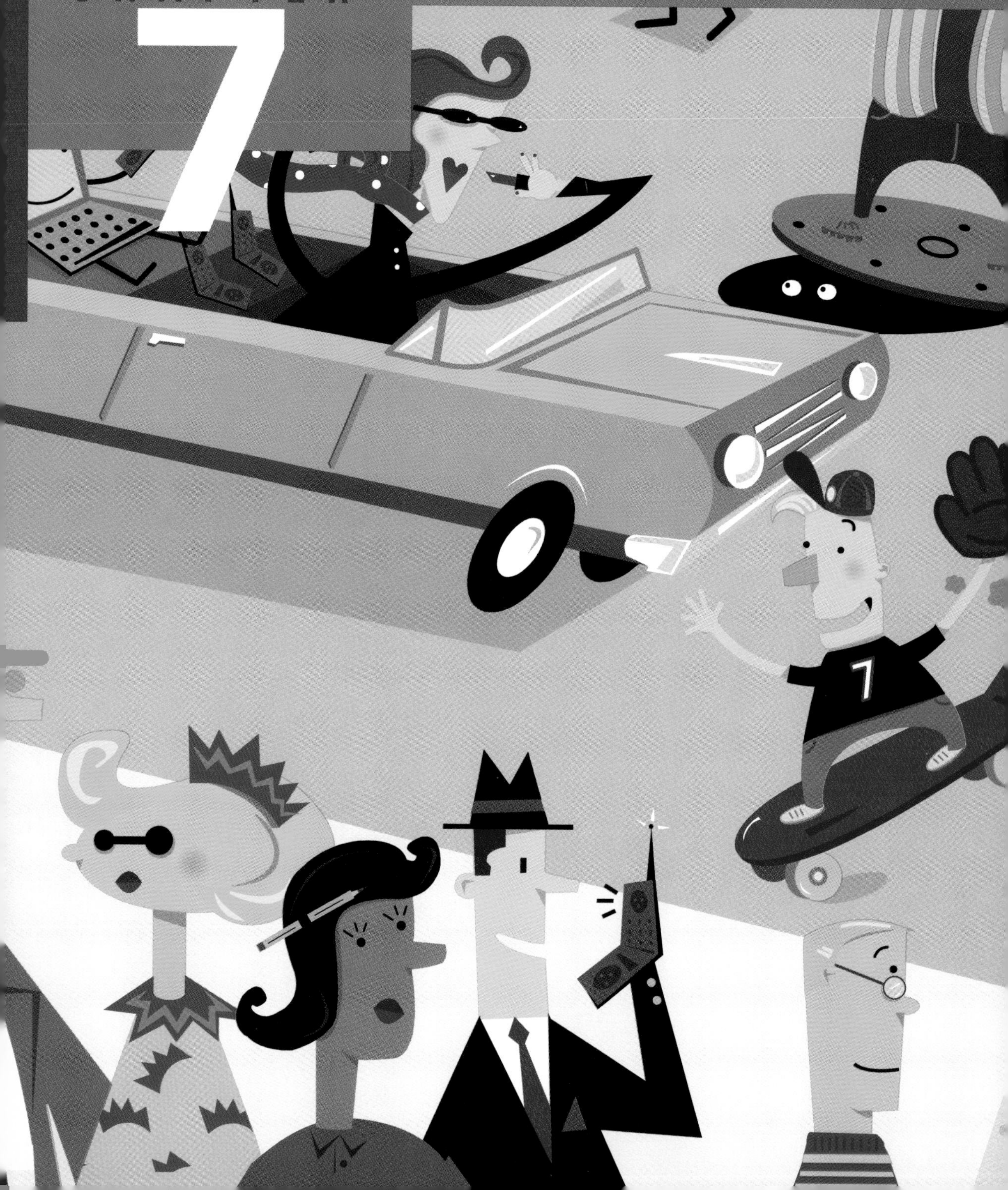

# An Introduction to Functions

# FAST FORWARD

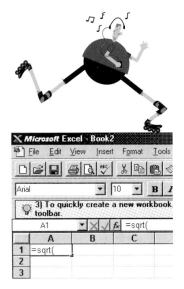

## MANUALLY APPLY FUNCTIONS ➤ *pp 133-135*

1. Functions can "stand-alone" in a cell, or be included as part of a larger formula in a cell.
2. Either type the function's name and an opening parenthesis, or pick the function's name from the list reached via the Insert menu's Function command. (If you manually type a function at the beginning of a formula, type **=** first.)
3. Either type necessary arguments or point to cells containing the arguments and click to include them.
4. Be sure to include necessary closing parentheses and any required commas as prescribed in online help for the particular function you are using.
5. Press ENTER to complete a function entry.

## GET WORKSHEET FUNCTION HELP ➤ *pp 135-137*

- For help with a specific function, type the function's name in the Help Index tab.
- For an overview of functions by category, visit the Index tab in Excel's Help system and enter the name of a category, then double-click the topic index of functions.
- For help while in the Function Wizard, click the Help button.

## USE THE FUNCTION WIZARD ➤ *pp 137-139*

1. Activate the cell where you want to place the function.
2. Click the Function Wizard button on the Standard toolbar.
3. Click to choose a category.
4. Click on a function's name to read about it.
5. When you find the desired function, be sure it is highlighted (click on its name) and click Next.
6. The Wizard will ask you to provide arguments for the function. If you don't know what to enter, click to select the blank in question, then click the Wizard's Help button.
7. When finished answering questions, click the Finish button.
8. Add to or edit the rest of the formula if necessary, then press ENTER to finish the formula.

**E**xcel's worksheet functions are built-in formulas that you can insert into cells and use to perform complex computations. Excel has hundreds of functions that facilitate engineering computations, manipulate text, and do much, much more.

Worksheet functions can often be used by themselves as stand-alone formulas, or they can be built into more complex formulas of your own creation. Before functions can do their thing, you need to provide data (*arguments*) that they will use in the computations. For instance, the SQRT( ) function finds the square root of a positive number. But the square root of what number? In the simplest case, you could type the formula =SQRT(9) into a cell and see the results (3). Or you could include the square root function in a more complex formula like =SQRT(9)*9.

Functions can often refer to places in your worksheet. For instance, =SQRT(A2) would compute the square root of the contents of cell A2. If you use named items in your worksheets, functions can sometimes refer to them as well. For example, =SQRT(VOLTAGE) might be a legitimate formula if your worksheet contains a positive number named VOLTAGE or some other formula that computed voltage. See Chapter 6 for information about names.

Some functions *inspect* things and take actions based on what they find. For example, the function ISNONTEXT( ) can check a cell and tell you if the cell contains text or not. Other functions *convert* things. The text function LOWER( ) converts text to all lowercase, for instance. The engineering function CONVERT( ) transforms values from one unit of measure to another (Fahrenheit to Celsius, feet to meters, and so on). Most functions are already installed with Excel. Others (like CONVERT) may need to be installed as *add-ins*. You'll see how that is done later in this chapter.

## PARTS OF A FUNCTION

Functions consist of *function names* and (usually) *arguments*. For instance, SQRT is the function name, while the value (the positive number) being evaluated is the argument. As you saw earlier in the square root example, arguments can be values, references, or names.

*Don't confuse worksheet functions with Excel's 400+ macro functions, which are discussed in Chapter 10. This chapter deals only with worksheet functions.*

*If you type a function as the beginning of a longer formula, or if the function is the only formula in a cell, you should precede the formula with an equal sign. As you will see later, if you use the Function Wizard, the wizard does it for you.*

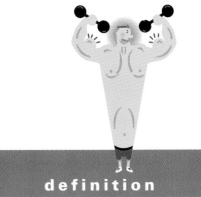
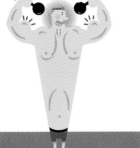

**Syntax:** *An agreed-upon method for describing and constructing computer instructions.*

They can also be text, logical values (TRUE and FALSE), or arrays. A function's *syntax* is a description of all the function's *argument names* in the order they should be used. For example, you might see the functions and their arguments expressed as

```
SQRT(number)
```

or

```
SUM(number1,number2...)
```

or

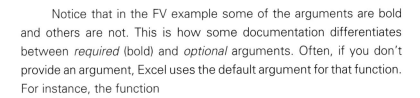

Notice that in the FV example some of the arguments are bold and others are not. This is how some documentation differentiates between *required* (bold) and *optional* arguments. Often, if you don't provide an argument, Excel uses the default argument for that function. For instance, the function

**DOLLAR(number,**decimals)

**CAUTION**

*The lesson here is that commas are important in functions, and that sometimes there is a big difference in the results if you delete a comma instead of leaving it and not entering an argument after it.*

converts numbers into text with dollar signs and, optionally, decimal places for cents. The expression =DOLLAR(200) would yield $200.00. (Notice the default decimal point and two places for pennies even though no second argument was supplied.) The expression =DOLLAR (200,1) would create the text string $200.0, and =DOLLAR(200,) would yield $200 (neither decimal point nor pennies). In the first example, leaving out the optional second argument *and the comma* that separates it causes Excel to use the default argument (a decimal point and two places, in this case). In the second example, the comma separates the second argument, which specifies the number of decimal places (1). In the third example, where there is a comma and no second argument, the comma suggests to Excel that there *is* a second argument (an argument specifying neither decimal point nor decimal places).

You can frequently use *other functions* as arguments. For instance, you could combine the ROUND and SQRT functions to compute the square root of a number, then round the results. The formula

```
=ROUND(SQRT(A1),2)
```

would compute the square root of the contents of cell A1, then round the answer to two decimal places.

# ONLINE FUNCTION HELP

If we described each Excel function in detail here, the book's size would quadruple, and its title would need to be changed to *Excel Function Reference for Busy Trivia Addicts*. Fortunately, you won't need to lug around some 600 extra pages of function minutia. Excel's extensive online Help feature and the Function Wizard will let you find and understand just the functions you're interested in. To expedite your searching, worksheet functions have been divided into up to 11 categories:

- Financial
- Date and Time
- Mathematical and Trigonometric
- Statistical
- Lookup and Reference
- Database
- Text
- Logical
- Information
- Engineering (optional and requires the Analysis ToolPak)
- User Defined (optional functions created by you or your programmer)

Use the Help menu's Microsoft Excel Help Topics command to get to the Index tab of the Help window. Then type **functions** and double-click on topics of interest.

To find out more about a specific function, go to the Answer Wizard tab of the Help Topics dialog box and type the name of the function. For instance, to learn more about the SUM function, you could type **SUM** at the top of the Answer Wizard tab, then click the Search button, and double-click SUM Worksheet Function in the scrollable topic list to go to that topic. If you'd rather browse, click on the Index tab and type the name of a function category, like "Financial" or "Statistical," or type the word **functions**, and pick the topic "worksheet function index."

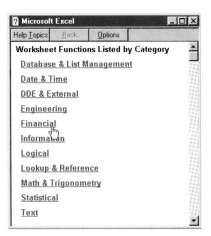

Since some of the help provided for functions is often fairly detailed and complex, you might want to print out the information that you find. Click the Options button in the Help windows and choose Print Topic.

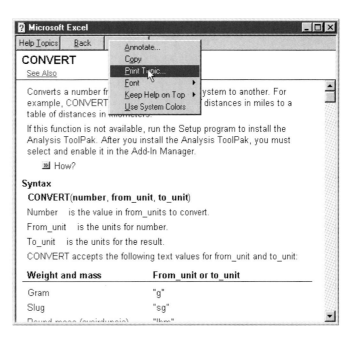

# THE FUNCTION WIZARD

The Function Wizard greatly simplifies the use of functions. It leads you through the necessary steps, shows the results as you work, and even provides examples of the functions in use.

1. Start by activating the cell where you want to paste the function.

2. If you need to begin your own formula before inserting the function, type it first, stopping when the insertion point reaches the place where you want to insert the function.

3. Click the Function Wizard button on the Standard toolbar, or choose Insert|Function. The Function Wizard's Step 1 window appears.

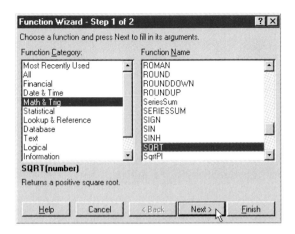

The Wizard lists functions within the categories mentioned earlier (Database, Date and Time, and so on). In addition, you'll see the Most Recently Used and All options.

4. Pick a category from the list on the left, then scroll through the list on the right to find the desired function.

5. Click to pick the function. Its name is displayed on the Formula bar and its name and arguments show near the bottom-left corner of the dialog box.

6. Read the wizard's description of the function to be sure it's the one you want.

7. Click the Next button and you will see the second Function Wizard dialog box.

## SHORTCUT

*The keyboard shortcut for the Function Wizard is SHIFT-F3.*

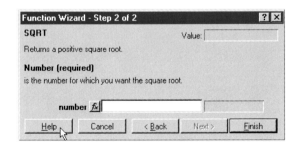

*Each dialog box is different and depends upon the function for its appearance and content. For instance, SQRT has only one argument, while PV has many.*

Here you see a list of arguments that are required and possibly some that are optional (and labeled as such). The arguments are explained onscreen, and the Help button provides real-life examples.

8. You can type directly in the wizard's entry boxes or use your mouse to point to cells containing the data you wish to use as arguments.

9. As you work, the wizard will show the results of its calculations in the Value area at the top-right corner of the dialog box.

10. Click Finish when your formula is complete. As you can see in Figure 7.1, when you click Finish, the wizard pastes the function into the active cell and displays the results of the current arguments in the cell. You'll see the formula in the Formula bar.

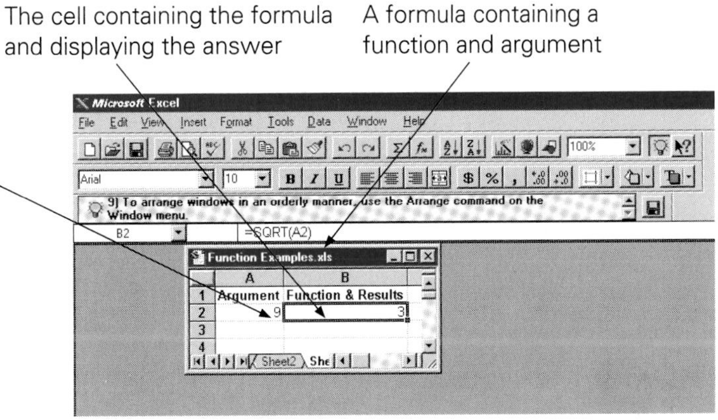

The cell containing the formula and displaying the answer

A formula containing a function and argument

The cell containing the argument data

**Figure 7.1** A function at work

*Entries can be the actual data (like the number 90), or cell addresses (like A1), or names (like SALES), or even other functions. Be consistent when entering arguments. For example, if you name the cell range A1:D12 SALES, don't use A1:D12 sometimes and SALES other times.*

# EXAMPLES OF FUNCTIONS BY CATEGORY

The best way to learn about functions is to experiment with them. Here are a few examples to get you started.

## Date and Time Functions

Some of the Date and Time functions simply *return* the current date and/or time. Others do date-and-time math. Let's first look at a function that finds and reports the current time—the NOW( ) function. When you use it, NOW( ) inserts (returns) a new serial number corresponding to the current date and time whenever the worksheet is recalculated.

For example, if you simply paste the formula =NOW( ) into a cell, it will display the current date followed by the current time, then update the cell's contents every time the worksheet is recalculated (and *only* when it is recalculated).

The actual *appearance* of cells containing the NOW( ) function (or other Date and Time functions) can be changed by using different date and time *types* found in the Number tab of the Format Cells dialog box, reached by choosing Format|Cells. For instance, Excel's Date format will display date and time in the format

```
m/d/yy h:mm
```

or in a number of other variations with or without the time. If you want to see only the *time* portion of a date serial number, format the cell(s) with one of five predefined time formats, or create your own.

Other Date and Time functions *compute* things using date serial numbers. For instance, the DAYS360 function computes the number of days between two dates, assuming a 360-day year (used by many accounting folks).

When you do any kind of date math, check your work very, very carefully. It is quite easy to produce technically correct answers that are not the ones you need. For instance, when computing working days, Excel does not automatically know that December 25th is a holiday for many folks. Your formulas will need to take things like this into consideration.

# Engineering Functions

Engineering functions are available, but require the Analysis Tool-Pak add-in macro, which you will probably need to install manually (i.e., get out your installation disks) if you didn't opt to install it when you first installed Office. Add the Pak using the steps described at the end of this chapter. The conversion function is a worthwhile addition to your collection. In the following illustration it is converting inches to millimeters.

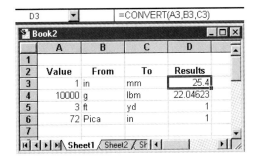

I used the Function Wizard to enter the function and answered three questions:

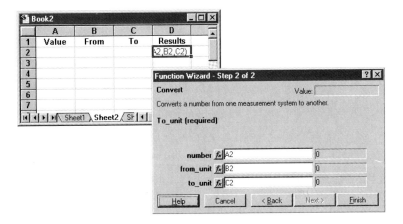

When I didn't remember how to specify the various units of measure, I looked up "convert" in the Index tab of Excel's online Help. The next illustration shows what information was available there.

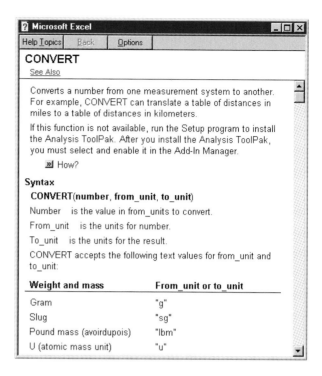

See how this all starts to fall together?

# Financial Functions

Excel's many financial functions are pretty well documented with online Help. Many of them can be used together or can be included as arguments, one within the other.

Here's an example of one way to use PMT, Excel's payment function. Officially, this function "returns the periodic payment of an annuity based on constant payments and a constant interest rate." In other words, it will tell you what your payments will be, given the loan amount, number of payments, and a fixed rate of interest. The function's syntax is

```
PMT(rate,nper,pv,fv,type)
```

The following image illustrates PMT at work.

*The Loan Manager template shipped with Excel uses the PMT function. You can see it at work by choosing the Loan Manager template from the Spreadsheet Solutions tab of the New dialog box. Click the Loan Amortization Table Tab, then select cell J16 (the first scheduled payment cell).*

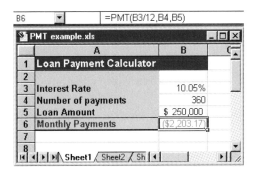

*Rate* is the interest rate *per period*. For instance, if you borrow at an annual fixed interest rate of 10.5% and then make *monthly* payments, the interest rate is 10.5% divided by 12. That explains the division portion of the formula above.

The argument *nper* needs the *total* number of payments. Thus, if you borrow for 30 years and make monthly payments, you'll make 30*12 or 360 payments. *Pv* is the present value, or total amount that the series of payments is worth now—the loan amount, in this case. Notice that in our example the optional *fv* (future value) and *type* arguments were omitted. *Future value* is a desired cash balance after the last payment is made. *Type* is either a 0 (zero) or 1. Omitting the *type* argument or entering **0** indicates that you will make payments at the end of each period. Entering **1**, on the other hand, tells Excel that the payments will be made at the beginning of the period.

Related financial functions include FV, IPMT, NPER, PPMT, PV, and RATE as separate functions.

# Information Functions

Some functions inspect things and report back. For example, ISEVEN( ) will let your formulas know if a cell contains an even number. Other information functions can check things external to Excel, like the amount of RAM in your computer, or which DOS version you are using. The next illustration shows INFO( ) at work. Its syntax is INFO(type).

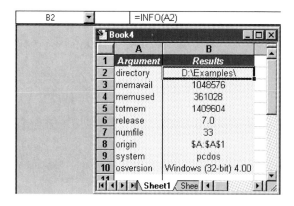

Cells B1 through B13 each have the same formula that refers to corresponding cells in column A, which contain the arguments that produce the results you see.

# Logical Functions

You use logic all the time. Chances are, you say things like "If I finish writing this chapter in time I can go out to lunch, otherwise I will nuke some frozen pizza." You can use logic in Excel, too. Take the IF function, demonstrated in Figure 7.2. Its syntax is

```
IF(logical_test,value_if_true,value_if_false)
```

It will help to look at a real-life example. The IF( ) function checks to see if the ending odometer reading is greater than the starting reading. If it isn't, chances are that the user has made a typographical error when entering readings. Or perhaps the odometer has reached its limit and "rolled over" to start again at zero. If the readings look okay, the IF function causes Excel to subtract the beginning from the ending readings (B3-B2). If there seems to be an error, the function displays text in the cell ("Check OD").

# Lookup and Reference Functions

Lookup and Reference functions go to cells you specify and return with answers. They can be used to create invoices that look up and insert different unit prices based on quantities purchased, for instance.

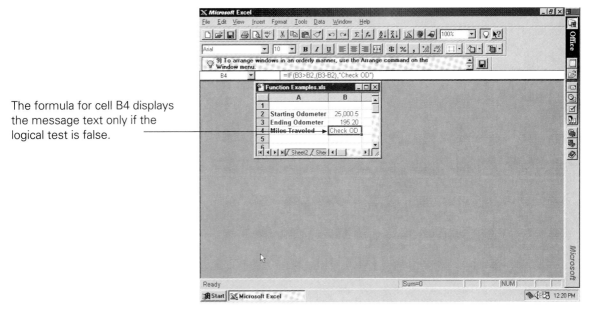

The formula for cell B4 displays the message text only if the logical test is false.

**Figure 7.2** Excel's IF function tests for conditions and does different things based on what it finds

These features can inspect rows, columns, or arrays. Take the simple example shown here:

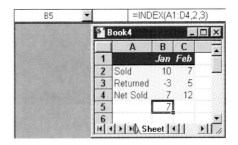

The INDEX( ) function here has been asked to go to the array bounded by cell addresses A1 through D4, then get the value stored in the cell three rows down and two columns across.

Lookup and Reference functions can refer to ranges, names, specific cell addresses, or row and column counts.

# Math and Trig Functions

You've already seen several of the Mathematical functions in action—RT( ) and SUM( ), for example. There are many others, enough to make an eighth-grade math teacher weep with joy. Most are quite straightforward, and well documented with online Help. Math and Trig functions can refer to cell references, names, or plain old numbers.

Two of the Math and Trig functions simply produce *numbers* whenever a worksheet recalculates. RAND( ) produces evenly distributed random numbers greater than or equal to 0 (zero) and less than 1 each time you recalculate—handy if you play the lottery or need to check probabilities. The PI( ) function inserts 3.141592654.

# Statistical Functions

Pollsters and statisticians will want to check out the many statistical functions, from AVDEV( ) to ZTEST( ). (AVDEV returns the average of absolute deviations, and ZTEST returns the two-tailed P-value of a z-test, don't cha know.)

# Text Functions

To manipulate or analyze strings of text in cells, use text functions. For example, CLEAN( ) will strip away any nonprinting characters stored in a cell. UPPER( ) converts text to all uppercase. DOLLAR( ) converts numbers to their spelled-out dollar equivalents and formats them in currency format.

# ERROR MESSAGES FROM FUNCTIONS

When you leave out or misuse arguments in functions, you will sometimes see cryptic error messages like "Error in formula," or a message like #NAME? or #NUM! will appear in the cell containing the flawed argument.

It is common to get messages like these when you work with names or text strings as arguments. Text strings *must* be enclosed in quotation marks, while names (references to areas, for instance) *must not* be in quotes. For instance, suppose you are using a math function like SQRT. If you enter the formula argument =SQRT(VELOCITY), Excel expects to be able to find a named numeric value or range of cells in your worksheet called VELOCITY. If it can't, you'll get the message #NAME? in the cell containing the formula. If you *do* have a positive numeric value named VELOCITY, the formula will use its contents as the function's argument. If the value of VELOCITY is negative, you'll see the error message #NUM!. Suppose you accidentally enclose the name VELOCITY in quotes, then try to use it as an arithmetic argument. The expression =SQRT("VELOCITY") will produce the error message #VALUE!, since SQRT needs a numeric value to do its thing, and material in quotes is treated as *text*.

# FUNCTIONS REQUIRING ADD-INS

Some functions require *add-ins*—additional software (such as a utility program) that is provided with Excel, but not automatically loaded when you run Excel. When you attempt to use functions that require add-ins, Excel loads the add-ins automatically for you. For example, the BESSELI and the DELTA engineering functions need the Analysis ToolPak. If Excel can't load the required add-in, it may be because you chose not to install add-ins when you initially installed Excel on your hard disk. Try rerunning the installer program to add these features. Here are the general steps for adding the Analysis ToolPak.

## Adding the Analysis ToolPak

1. Have your Excel or Microsoft Office installation disks or disc ready. (If using a CD-ROM, put it in the drive.) Quit any programs you are running including the Office toolbar.
2. Choose Settings and then Control Panel from the Start menu. Double-click the Add/Remove Programs icon in the Control Panel.
3. Click the Install/Uninstall tab if necessary to bring it forward.
4. In the resulting Properties dialog box click either Microsoft Excel or Microsoft Office, depending upon which installer disks or disc you are using.
5. Click the Add/Remove button in the Install/Uninstall tab.
6. Insert the first setup disk or your CD-ROM when prompted.
7. When you see the multibutton setup screen, click the Add/Remove button.

**CAUTION**

*It is important to perform step 10 or else the additional functions will not be available.*

8. If installing from the Microsoft Office disc or disks, click the Excel choice to select it and click the Change Option button.

9. Click the Add-ins choice and then the Change Option button.

10. Click in the box next to the Analysis ToolPak to place a check mark there.

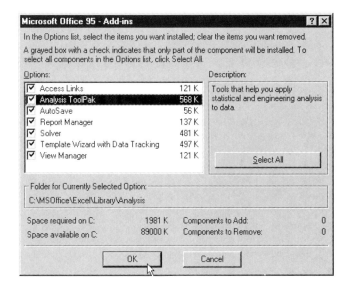

11. Click OK twice, then click Continue and follow the ensuing instructions. You should eventually be notified of a successful installation.

12. Choose the Add Ins command from Excel's Tools menu and place check marks in both analysis ToolPak boxes, then click OK.

# TO LEARN MORE ABOUT FUNCTIONS

There is clearly much more to know about Excel's functions. While you can learn a lot by experimenting and exploring Excel's online Help, you may also benefit from seeing all the functions in one place. Check out the *Microsoft Excel Function Reference* (at 500+ pages) shipped with the Excel program. Or, for a tutorial approach to the entire topic of functions, check out *Excel for Windows 95 Made Easy* by Martin Matthews (Osborne/McGraw-Hill, 1995).

# CHAPTER 8

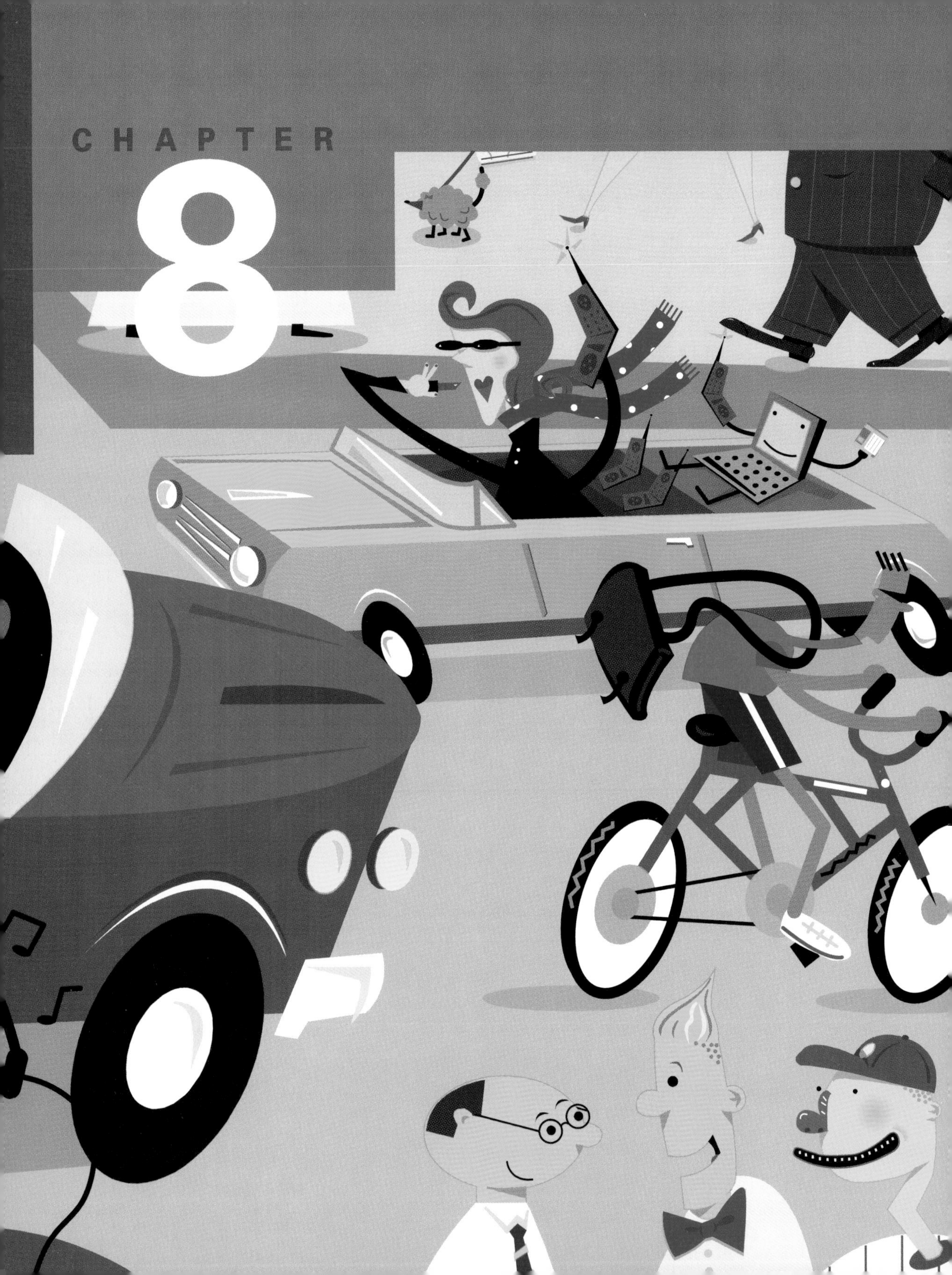

# Charts

# FAST FORWARD

## CREATE A CHART ➤ pp 156-158

1. Select the cells to be charted. Include labels.
2. Click the Chart Wizard button.
3. Drag a rectangle to indicate the desired size and shape of the graph object.
4. Answer the wizard's questions, clicking Next to move forward, Back to change your mind. (Watch the preview when you get to step 4.)

| Clear |
| --- |
| Insert Titles... |
| Insert Axes... |
| Insert Gridlines... |
| Insert Data Labels... |
| Format Chart Area... |
| Chart Type... |
| AutoFormat... |
| 3-D View... |
| Format Column Group... |

## CHANGE A CHART TYPE ➤ pp 158-160

1. Double-click on the chart to select it. It will be surrounded by thick, dark hashmarks.
2. Right-click and choose Chart Type from the shortcut menu.
3. Pick a new chart type and click OK or Options.
4. Resize the chart window if necessary to accommodate the changes.

## RESIZE A CHART ➤ pp 161-162

1. Click to select the chart object.
2. Drag with the size handles to resize the chart.

Forecast

## MOVE A CHART ➤ pp 161-162

1. Click once anywhere in the chart to select it.
2. Drag with your mouse.
3. Release the mouse button.

## ADD NOTES AND ARROWS ➤ *pp 162-164*

- Use the Text button in the Drawing toolbar to add text. (Click the Drawing button on the Standard toolbar, if necessary, to bring up the Drawing toolbar.) You'll need to click and drag to define the position, size, and shape of the text box.
- Use the Arrow button in the Drawing toolbar to add arrows.
- Double-click text boxes and arrows to change their appearance.

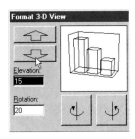

## ROTATE 3-D CHARTS ➤ *p 166*

1. Double-click a 3-D chart to display thick hashmarks around it.
2. Right-click anywhere in the chart.
3. Choose 3-D View from the Shortcut menu.
4. Click the Elevation and Rotation buttons to change the point of view.
5. Use the Apply button to see the results without closing the dialog box.
6. Click OK when satisfied.

## PRINT CHARTS ➤ *p 168*

- Charts print automatically when you print your worksheets.
- To inhibit automatic printing, remove the check mark from the Print Object option on the Properties tab of the Format Object dialog box. (Reach this box by choosing Format Object.)

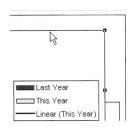

## DELETE CHARTS ➤ *p 168*

To delete a chart, click once on the chart to select it and press DEL.

**R**emember the old adage about how numbers can *lie*? Well, charts can *seduce*. Excel charts (which I often call *graphs*) make it easy for people to understand (or some would say, *misunderstand*) how data relate. It's one thing to write that a small percentage of our tax dollars go toward education; it's another thing to see a graphic representation of the relationship between education and defense expenditures. By the same token, if you create a 3-D bar representation of that same government budget, and rotate the chart just right, that little education bar looks bigger than it really is, and the defense bar looks smaller.

One of Webster's definitions of *seduce* is "to lead astray." Hmmm. Let's take a look at Excel's chart creation prowess.

# CHART PART TERMINOLOGY

Most busy people never learn the names of the various chart parts, and that's okay. But because there is plenty of online help available while you create and edit charts, and because that help refers to chart part names, you'll be much more productive if you take a moment to understand just a few concepts and terms.

## Chart Data Series

A *chart data series* is a collection of *related* values that are plotted on the chart. For instance, in the chart in Figure 8.1 there are three data series—the numbers in row 5 ($85,000, $80,000, and $88,000) make up the first series; the numbers in row 6 ($12,000, $28,000, and $30,800) make up the second data series; and finally, the numbers in row 7 ($106,000, $119,500, and $131,450) make up the third series.

## Data Markers

*Data markers* are the bars, pie wedges, dots, pictures, or other elements used to represent a particular data point (a single value in a series).

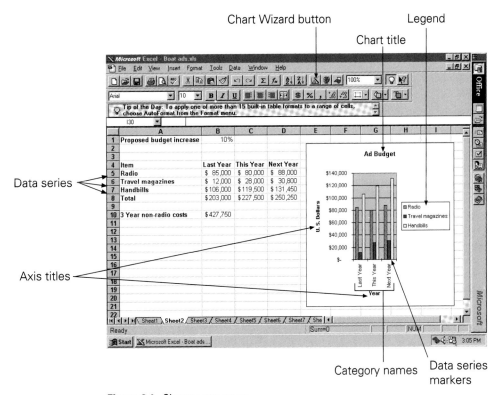

**Figure 8.1** Chart part names

For instance, the nine shaded columns in Figure 8.1 are each separate data markers.

When charts have more than one data series, the markers for each series usually look different. This is also illustrated in Figure 8.1, where the Radio columns are blue (or a shade of gray or a pattern when viewed on monochrome screens), while Travel magazine columns are red, and the Handbills columns are yellow.

It is also possible to use different *types* of markers for different series in the same chart. You might, for instance, use *columns* for one series and *lines* for another.

## Axes

An axis is a reference line denoting one of the dimensions of a chart. Excel can plot in up to three axes: X, Y, and Z. Usually the X-axis runs horizontally (left to right) and the Y-axis runs vertically (bottom to top). For instance, in Figure 8.1 the years run along the X-axis and the dollars run along the Y-axis. In three-dimensional charts, the Z-axis runs vertically, and the X- and Y-axes are at angles to display perspective.

## Category Names

*Category names* usually correspond to worksheet labels for the data being plotted along the X-axis (horizontally along the chart). For instance, in Figure 8.1 the category names are Last Year, This Year, and Next Year. The Chart Wizard identifies and includes category names when it creates a new chart. Some chart types place category names on the Y-axis.

## Chart Data Series Names

*Chart data series names* usually correspond to worksheet labels for the data being plotted on the Y-axis. For instance, in Figure 8.1 the chart has three data series names, one for each series. Data series names are usually displayed in a box (called a *legend*) alongside a sample of the color, shade, or pattern used for each data series. The Chart Wizard automatically identifies data series names and creates legends.

## Tick Marks and Grid Lines

Tick marks are short lines that intersect an axis to separate parts of a series scale or category. You can also add optional, longer grid lines in any of a chart's dimensions by selecting an axis mark and using the Tick Mark Type portion of the Patterns tab. Horizontal grid lines are illustrated in Figure 8.1.

## Chart Text

The Chart Wizard automatically adds text for things like the chart title and data labels. It is also possible to add your own text, like text boxes containing notes. Chart text is discussed later in the chapter, because by now you must be itching to create a chart. Let's cut to the chase.

# INSTANT CHARTS WITH THE CHART WIZARD

The Chart Wizard "looks" at the data you've selected to plot. It also "watches" as you drag to define the size and shape of the desired chart area. Next, it offers you a number of chart styles, and even lets you define chart titles. Faster than you can say "humuhumu" (the nickname of the Hawaiian state fish), you'll have a great-looking chart. Here are the steps for a simple column chart, plus some insights into the other options you'll encounter along the way.

# Starting and Assisting the Wizard

Start by creating a worksheet containing the data you wish to chart. In Figure 8.2 the cells A4 through D7 contain the necessary data and labels for a multiseries chart.

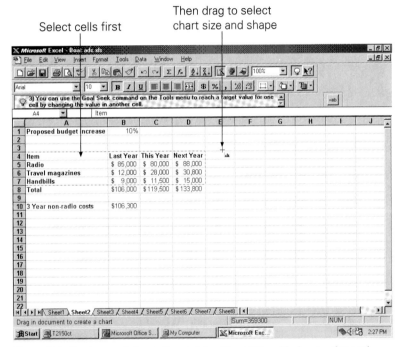

**Figure 8.2** Start a worksheet, then let the Chart Wizard help you size and shape it

1. Select the data to be included in your chart (probably most easily done by dragging to highlight the relevant cells). Don't include empty rows or columns or totals.

2. Click on the Chart Wizard button, shown here.
3. Marching ants surround selected cells, and your pointer turns into crosshairs with a little chart trailing it around as shown in Figure 8.2.

4. Drag with it, let's say from about E4 to around J20, to define the size and shape of your new chart. (To create a square, hold down the SHIFT key while you drag.)

5. When you release the mouse button, you will see the first of five Chart Wizard Step dialog boxes, shown here:

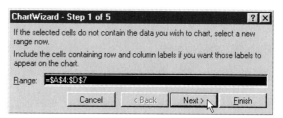

This box shows you the range of the data to be charted and gives you a chance to alter the selected range.

6. Normally, you'll click the Next button at this point, taking you to Step 2 of 5.

## Picking the Right Chart Type

The Chart Wizard can create many different *chart types* and many different *formats* for each of those various types. The Step 2 window, shown here, illustrates all the chart types and proposes one (Column, in our example).

**habits & strategies**

*Column, line and bar charts are great for plotting more than one series over time, while pie charts work best for a single data series where each part's proportions matter.*

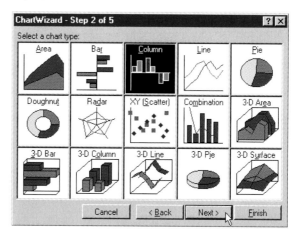

It's usually obvious from the chart samples which ones are best for various projects. You can also just experiment, or read online Help for each chart type. Use Help's Find feature to find information by chart type name (Radar, for instance).

*Watch the preview as you work.*

*Think about the general*

*presentation of the data at this*

*point. Does the chart help you*

*understand the data? Correct*

*axis? Nice chart type? If not, use*

*the <Back button.*

When you've decided on a chart type, click its sample to highlight it, then click the Next button to continue. Don't worry if you pick the wrong type; you can easily change it later. You might want to change the data series from Rows to Columns at this point as well.

Once you've chosen a chart type, the Chart Wizard presents a Step 3 dialog box showing various formatting options, which are different for each chart type. Here are the formatting options for column charts.

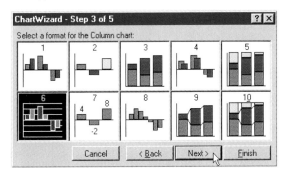

Don't lose any sleep over these choices, either. Formats can be easily changed later. Start with the choice the Wizard suggests, and experiment after you've seen those results. Click the Next> button to continue.

In Step 4, you'll see the beginnings of your chart design in a Sample Chart box. If you like what you see, forge ahead. Don't worry about the actual shape of the chart at this point, and don't be alarmed if your labels are temporarily truncated (shortened) or replaced with words like "Series 1" and "Series 2."

As you'll soon see, the settings proposed by the Chart Wizard are just fine for this sample project.

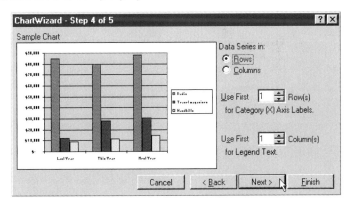

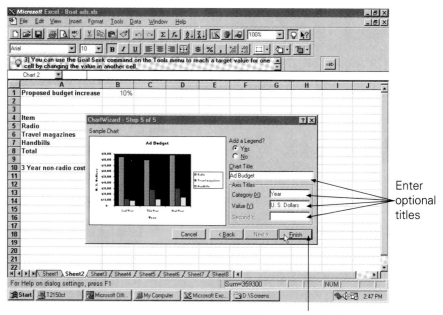

Enter optional titles

Click to create the chart

**Figure 8.3** Add optional titles and legends, then click the Finish button

You're almost done. Click Next again. Step 5 gives you a chance to add chart titles for the chart itself, and for each axis. You will see the titles appear in the Sample Chart area as you type. The Add a Legend? option turns legends on and off. Figure 8.3 shows the Step 5 dialog box.

If you change your mind before you click Finish, you can still go back to choose other options. When you click Finish, Excel will create a chart worksheet quicker than you can say "tourist" (the *real* Hawaiian state fish).

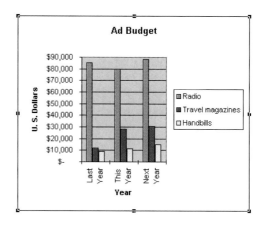

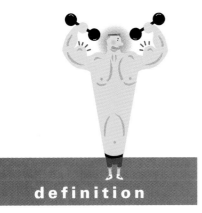

**d e f i n i t i o n**

*Linked Object: Objects (charts, text, drawings, etc.) which are not a part of the actual file you are using. Rather, they are stored elsewhere and your document "remembers" their location and "uses" their contents.*

# CREATING CHARTS ON SEPARATE WORKSHEETS

Excel charts can either be an integral part of your current worksheet or they can be separate *chart worksheets* in the workbook that are *linked* to selected worksheet data. The Chart Wizard usually creates chart objects on your current worksheet. The whole process is simple, clean, and automatic. But if you like, you can place charts on their own worksheets within a workbook.

## Separate Chart Worksheets

To create a new chart on a separate worksheet:

1. Select the data to be charted.
2. Choose Insert|Chart|As New Sheet.
3. You'll see the Chart Wizard. Use it as previously described.
4. The wizard will create a new sheet with a tab containing the word *Chart* and a sequential number.
5. Each new chart you create this way gets its own worksheet in the current workbook, and thus its own tab. Rename tabs just as you do any others—double-click on the tab.

# RESIZING AND MOVING CHARTS

You may need to change the size or shape of a finished chart, which is easily done by dragging the little black handles (squares) that surround a selected chart like the one shown in Figure 8.4.

One of eight handles →

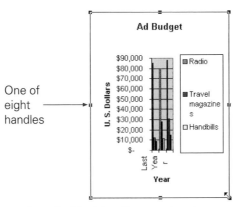

**Figure 8.4** Drag the black handles to resize charts

Besides making room for previously cramped labels, resizing a chart changes its size and shape, and thus the appearance of the data markers and other chart elements. Resizing is particularly useful if your data labels are invisible or all scrunched up. As you can see in Figure 8.4, though, resizing a perfectly nice chart can make it unreadable!

# ADDING CHART NOTES AND ARROWS

Often it's nice to be able to draw attention to, or explain, certain items on your chart. Here is an example of how to do this.

## ADDING A NOTE step by step

1. Display the Drawing toolbar if it is not already onscreen. (Click the Drawing button on the Standard toolbar, or right-click on a toolbar and choose Drawing from the shortcut menu).

2. Click on the Text Box button (it looks like a printed page).

3. Drag to create the outline of a text box in the approximate desired position, size, and shape.

4. Type and edit your note using text-editing techniques that should be familiar to you by now.

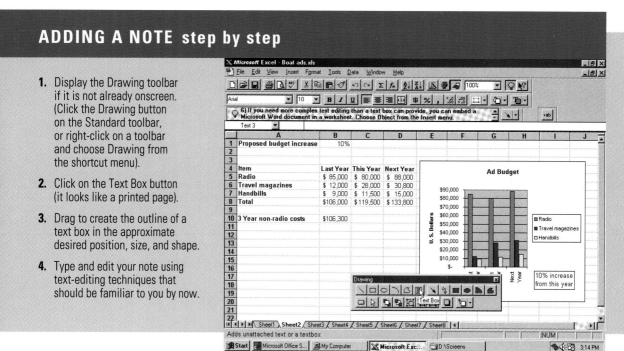

## Restyling and Resizing Text Boxes

To resize a text box or move it, point and click on any edge. The outline will thicken and you'll see eight size handles. Drag and resize this outline as you do any similar Windows object.

*If you want to add a drop shadow, an easy way to make one is to select the text box and click the Drop Shadow button on the Drawing toolbar.*

To embellish text, select it and use the Formatting toolbar or text-related menu commands. For instance, you might select text and then use the Bold toolbar button to make it bold.

To change the outline or fill pattern used for the box, or to add a drop-shadow effect, double-click on the edge of the text box. You'll see the Format Object dialog box shown here.

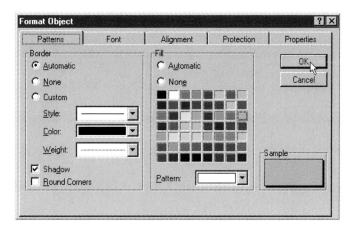

Choose the desired tab and options within the tab. For instance, the example shows the Shadow option being added via the Patterns tab.

## Drawing and Formatting Arrows

To draw an arrow:

1. Click the Standard toolbar's Drawing button, shown here, to display the Drawing toolbar.
2. Click the Drawing toolbar's Arrow button, shown here.
3. When your pointer turns into crosshairs, point where you want the arrow to *start* and drag to the *ending* point.
4. When you release the mouse button, an arrow will appear. You can drag either end of the selected arrow to reposition it and/or change the length of the line.
5. Double-click exactly on an arrow to bring up the Format Object dialog, which lets you define arrow styles, line thicknesses, colors, and much more.

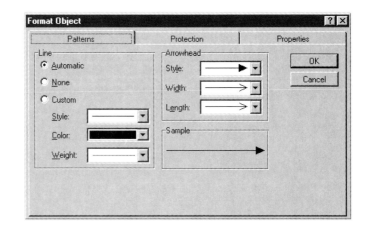

6. This changes only the arrow that you've double-clicked upon. To reformat other arrows immediately afterwards, select them (by SHIFT-clicking, perhaps), and use the Repeat Format Object command on the Edit menu.

# EDITING CHARTS

You could either get a life or spend the rest of your life exploring Excel's chart options. These are nearly endless. It's possible to change chart types and formats, embellish text, choose patterns or colors, add grid lines, and much more. Here's the quick tour of Excel chart voodoo.

You must first activate the chart for editing. You do this by double-clicking on the chart. You'll know you've succeeded when you see the thick "cross-hatch" lines, as opposed to the thin lines you get when clicking once.

## Changing Chart Types and Formats

Once you've created a chart, you can quickly change its type by clicking on the chart type list on the Chart toolbar. This provides a palette of chart choices that can be "torn-off" if you like and moved to a convenient spot on your screen for repeated use. Do this by dragging any edge of the list.

## Changing Data Series Ranges

There are several ways to change the data series ranges. One is to select a chart, then click on the Chart Wizard button. You'll see step 1 of a 2-step procedure. The first step lets you specify a new data range by typing it or dragging with your mouse. The second step lets you change the appearance of the chart.

# Selecting and Editing Chart Elements

You can edit specific parts of a chart, like text, grid lines, the shading used for markers, and so on, by simply double-clicking on them. For instance, to change the appearance of a chart title you would double-click on it to bring up the Format Chart Title dialog box.

To select the *entire chart*, click anywhere outside of the plot area, but not on other items like titles or legends.

To edit the content of the title object, click once to select the object, then select the text by dragging or waiting a moment before clicking or double-clicking on the text.

To select a *data series*, click on any marker in the series. For instance, to select the Radio spending series in your sample chart, you could click on any of the Radio columns in any year. You will then see a description of the data series in your Formula bar, where you can edit the series definition if you choose.

To select a *single data marker* (like the Last Year column marker in your sample chart), click on any marker in the series to select the series, then click on one of the markers in the series to select that marker.

To select a *grid line*, click exactly on a grid line. Clicking on any *axis* selects it. To select just the *plot area* (the columns without their category names, for instance), click in any part of the plot area not occupied by other things like grid lines or markers.

# More Formatting Techniques

Frequently, you can double-click on chart elements to quickly bring up relevant formatting options. If you double-click on a data marker, for instance, you'll soon see a Patterns dialog box that will let you select a new color or pattern for the marker. Double-clicking on a legend takes you to a dialog box where you can rearrange the appearance of the legends, and so on.

The other general editing technique is to select something, then use the appropriate menu commands and toolbar buttons.

## SHORTCUT

*The right mouse button reveals a number of chart-related choices if you point and click on a chart. This is often the quickest way to edit charts.*

## habits & strategies

*When in doubt, double-click.*

# ROTATING 3-D CHARTS

As you experiment with 3-D charts, you will find that in some instances tall parts of a chart will obscure inner details. Other times you'll just want to tilt or rotate a 3-D object to get a more dramatic effect. In either case, select a 3-D chart, then:

1. Right-click the chart.
2. Choose 3-D View from the shortcut menu.
3. You'll see a dialog box like the one in Figure 8.5. Use the Elevation buttons to tilt the chart and the Rotation buttons to rotate it. Use the Apply button to preview your changes in your chart without closing the dialog box. (Drag the dialog box if it gets in your way.) Clicking OK applies the latest changes and closes the box.

## CAUTION

*Tilting and rotating can really distort the relative size of neighboring data sets. (Or was that your intent?)*

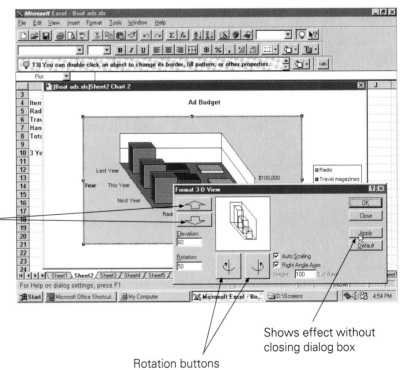

Elevation buttons

Shows effect without closing dialog box

Rotation buttons

**Figure 8.5** Try a 3-D chart to reveal inner details or to achieve a special effect

# CHANGING WORKSHEET VALUES BY DRAGGING CHART PARTS

Suppose you want to create a draft forecast that "looks" fair. That is to say, you want the numbers to look proportional, perhaps as a starting point for a budgeting discussion. Here's a neat way to "what if," or to make your data fit a desired scenario:

1. Create a worksheet and a chart.
2. Double-click to select the chart.
3. Click once on the data marker you wish to resize (the Last Year Radio bar in this example), then wait a second or two so as not to make Excel think step 3 is a double-click.
4. Click once again in the resulting square box in the marker (after that brief pause just mentioned).
5. Only the data marker you clicked on will be selected, and it will have some small, black selection markers.

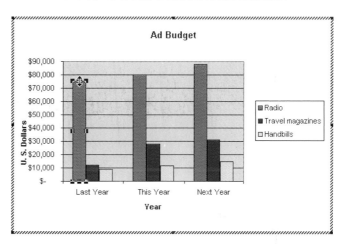

6. When you *drag* on the top-center black marker, you will be able to move that selected part of the chart *and* automatically change the numbers in the corresponding worksheet cell(s)! Watch the Name box to see the numbers change as you drag.
7. And, get this. When you release the mouse button, the number in the spreadsheet cell will change to match the graph.

*I can hear the voice of corporate America now: "Mary, make the report say we sold 60,000 units in December, truth be damned."*

# PRINTING CHARTS

Unless you tell Excel to do otherwise, it prints all charts. To display but not print an embedded chart, select the chart by single-clicking (don't double-click), then remove the check mark from the Print Object option on the Properties tab of the Format Object dialog box. Reach this box by choosing Format|Format Object.

If a chart is a separate worksheet, print it like any other Excel worksheet. Use the Page Setup and Print Preview features to format these documents, add headers or footers, and so on.

# DELETING CHARTS

To delete charts, simply select them and press DEL. If you delete a chart by mistake, Undo works here if you act promptly.

Delete separate *chart worksheets* as you would any other unwanted Excel worksheet. (Use the Delete Sheet command on the Edit menu.)

# SETTING THE DEFAULT CHART TYPE

The Chart Wizard and the New Chart (F11) command normally create new charts using the Column chart type and format 6. This is the default *preferred chart style*. You can define a different preferred style this way:

1. Double-click to select a chart from the current worksheet that you would like to use as the default. You'll see thick "crosshair" lines surround the chart.
2. Select Options from the Tools menu.
3. Click the Chart tab.
4. Click on the Use the Current Chart button in the Default Chart Format area.
5. Give the chart a custom format name in the resulting dialog box.

# CONTROLLING WHICH SERIES IS ON WHICH AXIS

Excel considers the numbers of rows and columns you've selected when determining how to plot your data. While space prohibits showing each chart type and examples of the results with different row/column combinations here, it's easy to watch the sample as you work with the Chart Wizard and change the outcome. For example, look at this:

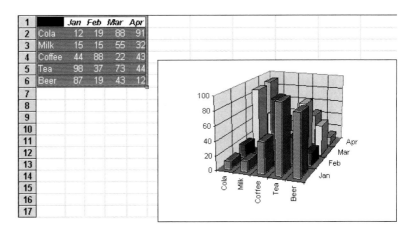

As you can see, Excel has plotted the months on the X-axis and the departments on the Y-axis because of the number of rows and columns selected. To overrule this choice, simply change the Data Series in: choice from Columns to Rows when the Chart Wizard asks. You can either do this while you are creating the chart, or later select the chart, then click on the Chart Wizard button and choose the Next> button to continue. Here is the same data plotted with the Data Series set to Rows.

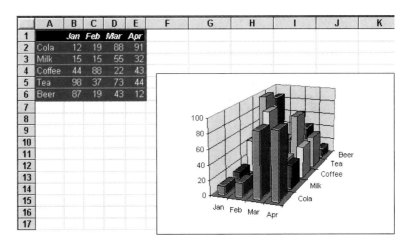

# ADDING OVERLAY CHARTS

Sometimes you'll want to overlay one kind of chart data on top of another. For instance, you might want to display the projected ad expenditures as a line over the prior and current year bars:

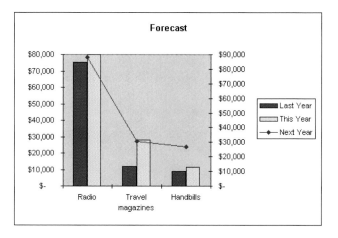

The easy way to do this is to choose the Combination chart type. It creates two *layers* on the chart, displaying half of the layers as bars and the other half as lines. If there is an uneven number of series, the extra series is plotted as bars.

# CREATING TRENDLINES

Trendlines are used to plot the direction of data in a series. It's easy to add trendlines to Excel bar, column, area, and scatter charts. To create trendlines on charts, follow these general steps (we'll use a simple exercise to demonstrate the technique):

1. Double-click on a chart object if necessary to select it.
2. Select the data series for the trendline by double-clicking on one of its markers.

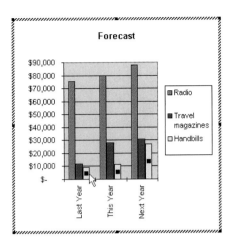

3. Right-click and choose Insert Trendline from the shortcut menu.
4. In the Trendline dialog box, pick a Trend/Regression type, as shown here.

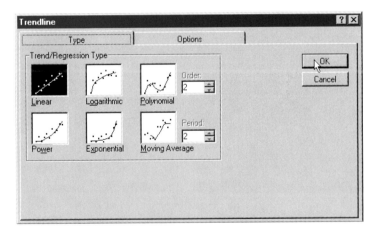

5. If necessary, click the Options tab of the Trendline dialog box and change options. For example, here we are extending the trendline for two periods to create a forecast.

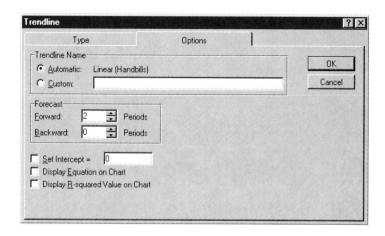

6. Click the OK button and admire your work or ask yourself what the heck you've done wrong.

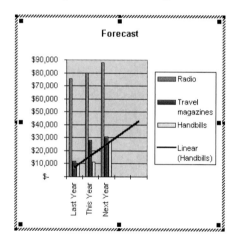

## CAUTION

*You might need to run the Excel or Microsoft Office Setup program to add the Data Map feature.*

# DATA MAP

Here's something guaranteed to spin their compasses in the board meetings. Excel has a terrific new feature called Data Map, which allows you to insert actual maps into your spreadsheets in lieu of the informative but not quite as snazzy charts and graphs. Figure 8.6 shows the Data Map window.

You can add titles, adjust shading, even draw demographics data from files on disk. Follow along here to learn how to make a data map.

Data Map toolbar

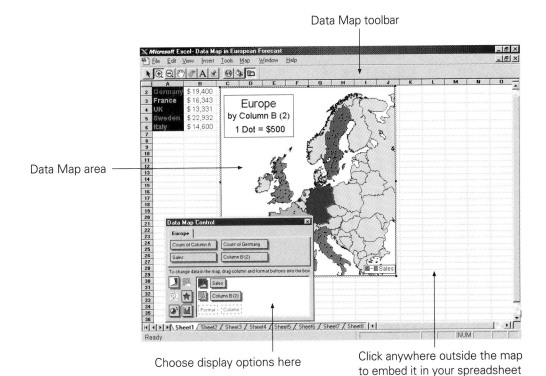

Data Map area

Choose display options here

Click anywhere outside the map
to embed it in your spreadsheet

**Figure 8.6** The Data Map window

# Using Data Map

To map data, follow these steps:

1. Select the data you wish to make into a map, and click on
   the Data Map button in the Standard toolbar.
2. Show Excel where you want your map to go by clicking
   and dragging.
3. After humming and whirring for a bit, Excel will open a new
   window and attempt to create the map, given the locations
   you have specified in your data.
4. Often Excel will have more than one map to choose from,
   so you might be asked to choose one. Notice there is a
   different toolbar in the Data Map window. If you use a
   country name that Excel doesn't know, you'll have the
   option to tell it the correct one.

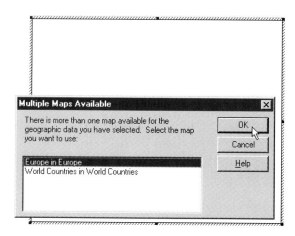

5. Excel will then place your map where you have specified and bring up the Data Map Control dialog box, where you can change shading along with many other options.

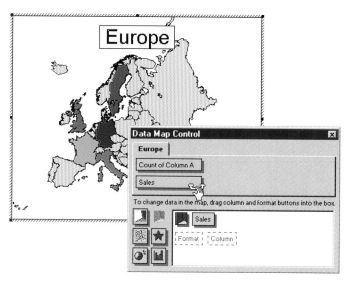

6. You now can accept the map as is or do a bit of editing, as explained in the next section. When you are satisfied with the map, click anywhere outside of it to embed it in your document.

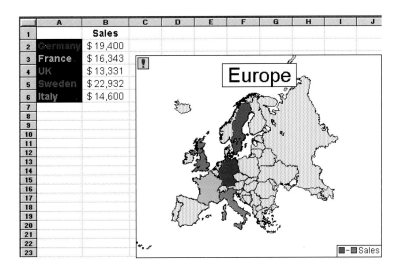

# Editing Maps

*You can double-click objects in maps (titles and such) and edit them just as you do Excel chart components.*

To edit a map, use any of the following techniques.

- Choose Insert|Data to bring up the Insert Data dialog box. Here you can specify what data should be included in the data map.

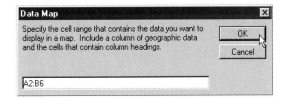

- You might want to have a closer view of your map, in which case, you can click on the Zoom button and click in the map.
- You can refresh the map at any time by clicking the Refresh button.
- To change the shading or format of a column's data, drag the column into the Format box of the Data Map Control dialog box and click on the appropriate button.
- To edit an existing map, just double-click on the map to get back to the map window.

**habits &
strategies**

*When you are editing a map, the
top command in the Help menu
is Data Map Help. It provides
extensive help for the Data Map
feature. Give it a visit.*

Here's what a typical finished map looks like:

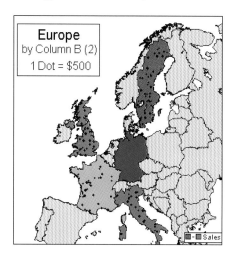

## Using Demographics Info

You can link your maps to demographics data that comes with
Excel in the file called Mapstats.xls, found in the Datamap folder. You
can then use this information along with your own sales results to
monitor trends and predict demand. See the big books on Excel for
more details.

## TELL ME MORE

These are the basics of Excel charting and, as you can see, skills
you learned in Windows and practiced in Word are often called for and
applied in Excel. Many times, just reading the menu, dialog boxes, or
the status bar will show you how to do new and useful things.

But there may be other charting details that are not so obvious.
For instance, you can link a chart's text with worksheet cells so that
chart notes or labels change when worksheet cells change. You can
sometimes plot nonadjacent data. There is more to know about forcing
axis values than you've read here. If you don't find the answer to
questions like these in Excel's online Help, check out the hundred-plus
pages on charts in your Excel manual, or pick up *Excel for Windows 95
Made Easy* by Martin S. Matthews (Osborne/McGraw-Hill, 1995).

# Graphics

# FAST FORWARD

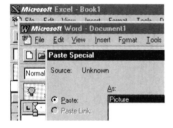

## IMPORT GRAPHICS ➤ *pp 182-183*

Either copy the graphic to your Clipboard, then paste, or use the Insert Picture or Insert Object commands.

## EXPORT GRAPHICS FROM AN EXCEL WORKSHEET ➤ *p 183*

To export a graphic created with the Drawing (or mapping) tool, select the graphic and place it on the Clipboard with the Copy command. (This will replace the previous Clipboard contents). Switch to the destination program and paste the graphic.

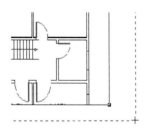

## MOVE A GRAPHIC ➤ *p 184*

1. Click to select the graphic.
2. Handles will appear indicating successful selection.
3. Click anywhere on the object except on a handle.
4. Drag the object and release the mouse button when you are happy with the positioning.

## RESIZE A GRAPHIC ➤ *p 185*

1. Click to select the graphic.
2. Handles will appear indicating successful selection.
3. Drag handles to resize. (Clicking corner handles resizes in both directions at once.)

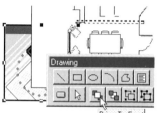

## SEND GRAPHIC ELEMENTS
## FORWARD OR BACK ➤ *p 185*

1. Select a graphic element (a picture or drawing part or whatever).
2. Use the Send To Back or Bring To Front buttons on the Drawing toolbar.
3. Repeated clicking on the buttons will move layered items further up or back when that is possible.

## DISPLAY THE EXCEL
## DRAWING TOOLBAR ➤ *p 185*

1. Click the Drawing button in the Standard toolbar.
2. Drag the Drawing toolbar to an out-of-the-way location.

## ADD LABELS ➤ *p 186*

1. Click the Drawing toolbar's Text Box button.
2. Drag to create the desired text box location, size, and shape.
3. Type the text.
4. Click outside the text box when you are done.
5. Double-click a finished text box to change its appearance (fill pattern, fonts, etc.).

## DRAW LINES AND ARROWS ➤ *pp 186-187*

1. Click the Line button in the Drawing toolbar to draw lines or the Arrow button to draw lines with arrowheads.
2. Click at the desired starting point to begin the line.
3. Drag to the desired ending point.
4. Double-click lines to change their appearance (thickness, color, etc.).

**H**ere's a quandary. You are in a hurry, but you want your presentation to be first-rate. Graphics can add interest to your worksheets. Sometimes they can even help people visualize your numbers. The trick is to not get so carried away that you miss your deadline, or make the worksheet look so busy that the art distracts from important numbers. Worksheets can include imported graphic images, items you draw yourself, arrows, text boxes, and so on.

Figure 9.1 is an example of a worksheet drawn from many sources: The calculator logo is from the Microsoft Office ClipArt folder, the price tag was drawn using Excel's Drawing toolbar, and the blueprint came from a program called 3D Home Architect. Prices of the individual remodeling options are entered into worksheet cells, and the *Total Cost* figure of $20,750 in the price tag is a worksheet cell containing a formula that adds up al the items.

# IMPORTING AND EXPORTING GRAPHIC OBJECTS

Excel 95 follows most of the Windows 95 graphics importing and exporting conventions. You can move things from place to place with your Clipboard, or by using Insert Picture, Map, and Object commands. You can place graphics anywhere on a worksheet. Select graphics to move, resize, and restyle them. Copies of Excel graphics can be pasted from your Clipboard into a worksheet or linked with the original objects so that changes in the original are reflected on the worksheet.

## Importing Graphics

As a general rule, if you can get a graphic onto your Clipboard, you can paste it into an Excel worksheet. There are several ways to include graphics:

- Paste from the Clipboard.
- Use the Picture command on the Insert menu.
- Use the Object command on the Insert menu.
- Use the Map command on the Insert menu for pasting maps.

Add text with text drawing tools          Click to show the drawing toolbar

Graphics can surround cells without hiding their contents

Draw your own graphics in Excel with these drawing tools

Add arrows

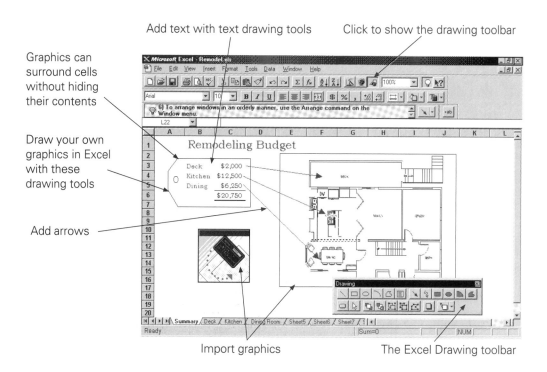

Import graphics          The Excel Drawing toolbar

**Figure 9.1** Import graphics or draw your own

Any of Microsoft's object-creating tools (WordArt, the ClipArt Gallery, etc.) can provide graphic images. Simply use the Insert Object command to bring up the available list of object creators, shown in the next illustration, then locate the desired graphical file.

## habits & strategies

*Frequently, it's best to use the Paste Special command rather than the Paste command or the CTRL-V keyboard shortcut when inserting graphics into worksheets. This creates a link so that when the original object is changed, the linked copy is updated.*

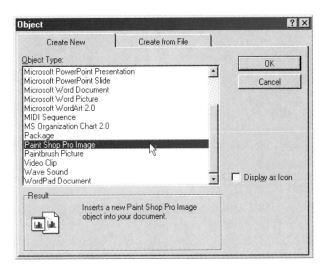

## SHORTCUT

*To align a graphic object's border with the worksheet cell grid, hold down the ALT key and drag one of the object's corner handles.*

# Exporting Excel Graphics

You can also paste parts of your Excel worksheet into other types of documents. For instance, you can copy an Excel drawing or chart to your Clipboard, then switch to another program and paste (or Paste Special) the Clipboard contents either as a picture or often in other formats. The type of pasting that you do and the program you paste into determine how the pasted items will both appear and behave in the destination document.

Chances are, you already know how to resize Excel graphics, but in case you need a refresher, check out the blue box on the next page.

# MOVING WORKSHEET GRAPHICS

To move an object, click to select it, point anywhere within the selected object, and drag with your mouse. To move more than one object, SHIFT-click on each of them. Drag them all at once with your mouse and release. You can also move graphics by selecting them, then copying or cutting them to the Clipboard, and pasting them elsewhere.

## RESIZING GRAPHICS step by step

1. Select a graphic by pointing with your mouse.

2. When the handles appear, drag on a handle to resize the graphic.

3. To change both dimensions at once, drag the corner handles.

4. Use Undo if you don't like the finished look of the object.

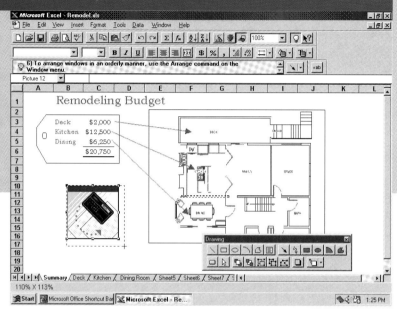

# Sending Graphic Items Forward and Back

Sometimes you'll want to move overlapping items in front of or behind each other. Select the item you wish to move and use the Drawing toolbar's Bring To Front and Send To Back buttons.

# DRAWING LINES AND SHAPES

Excel provides a number of drawing tools that work like most similar Windows-savvy drawing tools. Reach them by clicking the Drawing button, shown here, on the Standard toolbar.

Since you've probably used similar drawing tools by now, we'll not waste paper here covering what must be familiar ground. If you forget what a tool does, point to the tool in question and read its description in the status bar area. Incidentally, the polygon and oval tools were used to create the price tag in Figure 9.1.

*To learn more about drawing tools, visit the Find tab in the Help window and search for draw, drawing toolbar, or graphic.*

Drag to define the desired
text box size, then type

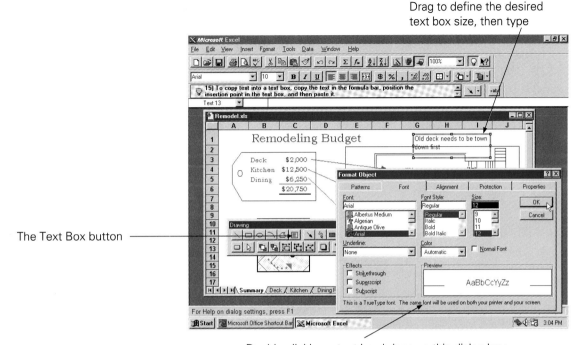

The Text Box button

Double-clicking a text box brings up this dialog box
where you change text appearance

**Figure 9.2** A small text box and the tools you use to work with text boxes

# ADDING LABELS TO GRAPHICS

To place text labels in your graphics, either type right in the empty
cells, or use the Text Box button on the Drawing toolbar. If you use the
latter technique, begin by clicking the Text Box button, then drag to
define the size and shape of the box that will contain the text. Next,
type in the resulting box. Click outside of the object when you finish
typing. Figure 9.2 shows an example of a text box and its related tools.

To change the appearance of a text box, double-click it. When you
see the Format Object dialog box, pick the appropriate tab (Patterns,
Font, etc.) and make the desired changes. Click OK when you are done.

# ADDING ARROWS AND LINES TO EXCEL GRAPHICS

To draw arrows on your worksheets (to point to parts of a graphic
object, for example), use the Arrow tool on the Drawing toolbar. It looks

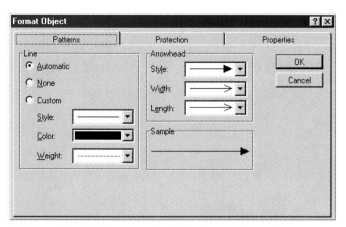

**Figure 9.3** Double-click, then use this dialog box to change the appearance of an arrow

like an arrow complete with arrowhead. To draw, click the Arrow tool button, then point to where the line will start (usually the non-arrowhead end) and drag to where you want the arrowhead to point, then release the mouse button. You should get a line and an arrow. To change the appearance of the arrow (line thickness, color, head style, etc.), double-click it. You'll see a dialog box like the one in Figure 9.3. Click OK when you are done.

# EXAMPLES OF GRAPHICS IN EXCEL

You can create invoices and other forms that include logos, as illustrated here.

| Three Foxes and a Ferry | Invoice No. |
|---|---|
| Pier 1 | Customize... |
| Sausilito Bay, CA 9400 | |
| 415.555.1234 | **INVOICE =** |

**Customer**

| Name | | Date | 9/11/95 |
|---|---|---|---|
| Address | | Order No. | |
| City | State        ZIP | Rep | |
| Phone | | FOB | |

| Qty | Description | Unit Price | TOTAL |
|---|---|---|---|
| | | | |

In this case, the Microsoft Invoice template came with a button that made it easy to insert the graphic. You start by opening an invoice template with the New command. Then switch to the Customize your Invoice tab and scroll to the bottom of the page where you will find the Select Logo button.

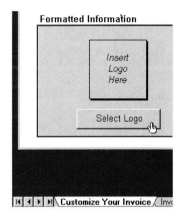

The button brings up the Open dialog box and lets you search for graphic files. When you find one you like, double-click it and Excel inserts the graphic and automatically resizes it to fit the space allotted on the template. (You'll need to switch back to the Invoice tab to see the finished product.) Very slick.

The same basic technique could be used to place illustrations in order forms.

And how about this? Excel makes a great teaching tool. Set up some spreadsheets that illustrate concepts and let students explore, as illustrated here.

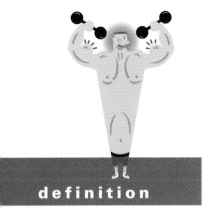

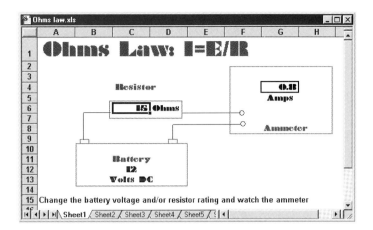

**OLE:** *Short for Object Linking and Embedding, this is Microsoft's way of letting you attach portions of one project to another. The things you attach are called objects and might be graphics, text, worksheet cells, multimedia files, you name it. See also: slowing your computer to a halt.*

# OTHER GRAPHICS YOU CAN INSERT

As I wrote earlier, if you can get it on your Clipboard, or if it comes from an OLE-savvy program, you can paste it into your Excel worksheet. Multimedia images and clips, WordArt, equations from Word's Equation editor (although you won't be able to compute equations pasted this way), organizational charts from Microsoft Organizer, Paintbrush pictures, items you scan with your graphic scanner, clipart from online services—the list goes on and on.

Compatible file types include Computer Graphics metafile (.CGM), Bitmap graphics (.BMP), Encapsulated PostScript (.EPS), Hewlett Packard Graphics Language—HPGL (.HGL), Lotus 1-2-3 graphics (.PIC), Micrografx Designer/draw (.DRW), Tagged Image File Format (.TIF), WordPerfect graphics (.WPG), PC Paintbrush (.PCX), CorelDRAW (.CDR), and Macintosh PICT files (.PCT). And remember, if you have programs that can convert graphic formats not mentioned here into formats which are mentioned here, you can get the item into Excel that way.

**upgrade note**

*Excel no longer offers a Slide Show feature. Guess they want you to purchase Microsoft Office and use PowerPoint. They're right. PowerPoint is a better tool for presenters than that old Slide Show feature.*

MAIL

# Introduction to Command Macros

# FAST FORWARD

## RECORD A MACRO ➤ *pp 195-199*

1. Pull down the Tools menu, point to Record Macro, and click on Record New Macro.
2. Type a name for the macro.
3. Click on Options.
4. Select the location for the macro in the Store In section. Choose Personal Macro Workbook to access the macro from any workbook.
5. Click on OK.
6. Perform the actions that you want to record.
7. Click on the Stop button.

## RUN A MACRO ➤ *p 199*

1. Pull down the Tools menu and click on Macro.
2. Double-click on the macro name in the list.

## ASSIGN A NEW MACRO TO
## THE TOOLS MENU OR KEY COMBINATION ➤ *p 200*

1. Pull down the Tools menu, point to Record Macro, and click on Record New Macro.
2. Type a name for the macro.
3. Click on Options.
4. To assign the macro to the Tools menu, click on the Menu Item on Tools Menu checkbox, then enter the menu text.
5. To assign the macro to a key combination, click on the Shortcut Key checkbox, then enter the key(s) in the box next to Ctrl+.
6. Click on OK and continue recording the macro.

## ADD A MACRO TO A TOOLBAR ➤ *pp 202-203*

1. Record the macro.
2. Right-click on any toolbar and choose Customize from the shortcut menu.
3. Scroll through the Categories list and click on Custom.
4. Drag the desired button to a position on a toolbar.
5. Double-click on the macro name in the list.
6. Close the Customize box.

## DELETE A MACRO ➤ *pp 203-205*

1. Pull down the Tools menu and click on Macro.
2. Click on the macro you want to delete.
3. Click on Delete.

To delete a macro from the Personal Macro Workbook, it must be unhidden.

## DISPLAY THE PERSONAL
## MACRO WORKBOOK ➤ *p 205*

1. Pull down the Window menu and select Unhide.
2. Double-click on Personal.xls.

To hide the workbook, display it onscreen and select Hide from the Window menu.

**S**uppose I told you that Excel offers a feature that will watch you do tedious, labor-intensive, detail-riddled tasks, learn how you work, and then automatically do the grunt work for you in the future. Sounds pretty handy, huh? And the feature doesn't require that you become a computer programmer. You can pick up the basics in a few minutes. Better yet, you can create specific solutions to unique problems, or general ones that can be used over and over on a variety of projects.

Too good to be true? Probably. Because, while Excel can watch and learn as you move the mouse and choose menus and make decisions, it cannot get inside of your head to know *why* you've done what you've done. And it doesn't know anywhere near as much about your project as you do, so it might blindly do things that made perfect sense in one project and not in another. In effect, when you use the techniques in this chapter you are putting your work into the hands of a really dumb, really quick servant. If there is a single chapter in the book to be approached with wide-eyed skepticism and extreme caution, this is it. The topic is *macros*.

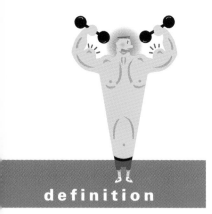

**definition**

*Macro: A collection of actions—keystrokes, menu and toolbar selections—stored together as one unit.*

# WHY MACROS?

We're creatures of habit. We develop patterns, ways of doing things that we repeat, if not out of habit, then for convenience. Perhaps you type the same heading on every worksheet, or have a special format that you like to apply to cells. Maybe there's a formula that you use often, or a certain template that you like to use. Rather than repeat a series of actions each time you want to perform them, you can record the actions in a macro.

Whenever you want to perform that task again, you just run the macro. You can select it from a list, or even run it by pressing a key combination, clicking on a toolbar button, or choosing it from a menu. In a sense, a macro is just like a shortcut key, button, or menu item that's already built into Excel. The only difference is that a macro performs the functions that *you* want it to perform.

Macros not only speed up your work with Excel, but they help you to be consistent and to avoid mistakes. Suppose, for example, that you're creating a series of worksheets on the annual budget. You want all of the worksheets to have the same look and feel, to share some common elements and design. Rather than try to remember what formats to apply, just create one or more macros to apply them for you.

## upgrade note

*Macros haven't really changed since Excel 5 for Windows. So if you're up to speed on macros, just scan over this chapter to refresh your memory.*

In this chapter, you are going to learn how to record *command macros*. A command macro is one that repeats keystrokes and mouse actions. Another type of macro, a *function macro*, lets you create your own functions. You can then use the functions you create just like the built-in ones that you learned about in Chapter 7. You can't record a function macro, you can only write one—something that a truly busy person might not have time for.

# RECORDING YOUR OWN MACROS

The quickest way to create a macro is to record it. All of the keystrokes and mouse actions that you perform are saved—recorded in the exact order that you do them.

Keep in mind that the steps you do to record the macro are actually performed whenever you run the macro. So before you record the macro, set up Excel so it is exactly how you'd want it to be when you later run the macro. For example, if you want to record a macro to insert a heading into a specific worksheet at the same time that you record the macro, open the workbook and display the sheet first (before you record the macro). If you open the workbook and display the sheet after you start to record, then those actions will be part of the macro itself.

When you're ready to record a macro, follow these steps.

## RECORDING A MACRO step by step

1. Pull down the Tools menu, point to Record Macro, and click on Record New Macro.

2. Type a name for the macro that represents the function that it will perform.

3. Type a description of the macro.

4. Click on OK.

5. Perform the actions that you want to record.

6. Click on the Stop button.

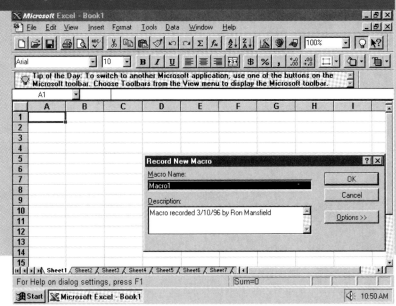

## habits & strategies

*The Description box will contain the date and your name. Many users are too busy to enter anything more, but you should take the time to enter a brief description of the macro.*

Let's create a macro now to see how these steps work. This macro will insert a new row at the top of the worksheet and enter a small heading. First, make certain that you have a blank worksheet on the screen, or one that you don't mind changing. Then pull down the Tools menu, point to Record Macro, and click on Record New Macro to see the Record New Macro dialog box.

Excel will imaginatively suggest a macro name for you—Macro1, Macro2, and so on. Rather than accept the name—who would ever remember what Macro23 performs?—type a name that illustrates the macro's function. Names must begin with a letter, and they cannot contain any spaces or punctuation marks other than the underline character. To make names readable, use uppercase letters or the underline character to indicate words, such as Print_In_Landscape, or EnterMyHeading. For now, type **MyHeading**.

Now click on OK so you can start recording the macro. When the dialog box disappears, you'll see the Stop Recording toolbar (although its full name doesn't show) with one button, the Stop Macro button. Now perform these steps to record the macro.

1. Press CTRL-HOME to move to cell A1. Do this anyway, even if you're already there. This records the keystroke so the macro will move to cell A1 if you run it from some other location.
2. Pull down the Insert menu and click on Rows. (Remember, one of our goals was to have the macro insert an additional row.)
3. Type **Submitted by**, followed by your name.

**CAUTION**

*Do not forget to stop recording. If you just continue working instead, all of your actions will be recorded.*

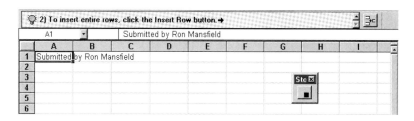

4. Click on the Enter button in the Formula bar. You can also press ENTER to accept the entry, but this also moves to the next row, recording the action in the macro.
5. Click on the Stop Macro button.

The macro is recorded and saved as part of the workbook (on a new worksheet titled Module 1, which will be inserted after the last existing worksheet). Now you can use it to insert a heading on any worksheet that's part of the workbook.

# Selecting a Macro Location

By default, Excel will record your macro in the workbook itself. This means that you'll only be able to run the macro when the workbook is open. If you want to use the macro with every workbook, then you must record it in the Personal Macro Workbook. When you record the macro, click on the Options command in the Record New Macro dialog box to expand it to see the options shown in Figure 10.1.

## CAUTION

*If you add a macro to the Personal Macro Workbook, when you exit Excel, a message will appear asking if you want to save the Personal Macro Worksheet. Select Yes if you want to save your macros stored there.*

*During an Excel session, the Use Relative Reference option stays on until you click it a second time. Be sure to deselect it if you want to return to an absolute reference. Quitting and restarting Excel also switches to absolute referencing.*

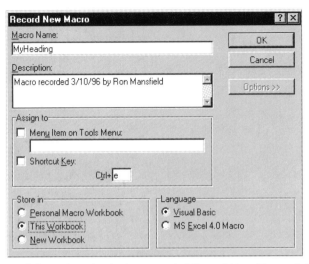

**Figure 10.1** Select a location in the expanded Record New Macro dialog box

To make the macro global for all workbooks, click on Personal Macro Workbook. This is a special workbook automatically opened, but not displayed on the screen, when you start Excel. It is stored in a file named Personal.xls in the XLStart subfolder found in your Excel folder, but the file will not exist until you create a macro there and save the personal workbook the first time.

You can also choose to record the macro in a new workbook. If you choose this option, Excel will open another workbook just to record the macro. However, you'll have to open the workbook before you can access its macros.

# Absolute and Relative Reference

Even "simple" macros can be tricky, and things can go haywire. One of the most common problems is caused by recording macros using absolute references, the default setting.

For example, suppose you use a series of column headings frequently, so you decide to record them in a macro. You start recording in cell A1, then enter the headings using the TAB key to move from column to column—from A1 to B1, C1, and D1. Then you stop recording to complete the macro. So far, so good.

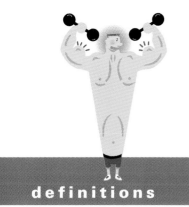

**definitions**

***Absolute Reference:*** *In the context of macros, absolute references instruct the macro to select the same cells each time the macro is run.*

***Relative Reference:*** *In the context of macros, relative references instruct the macro to select a cell relative to the macro's current position, not a specific cell.*

*If you store a macro in the Personal Macro Workbook, its name will be preceded by the notation Personal.xls.*

You're now ready to run the macro to enter the same headings elsewhere in the worksheet. So you move to cell C14, where you want the headings to appear, and then run the macro. What happens? The first entry appears in cell C14, but the others get inserted back in B1, C1, and D1 again. The absolute reference told Excel to insert the first heading and then move to cell B1, then C1, then D1. Not what you wanted. The solution is to record cell selections using relative references.

Before recording the macro to insert the column headings, pull down the Tools menu, point to Record Macro, and click on Use Relative References. Then record the keystrokes. Now when you run the macro starting in C14, the remaining headings will appear in D14, E14, and F14. The relative references told Excel to insert the first heading and then move one column to the right , insert the second heading and shift one more column to the right, and so on.

# RUNNING A MACRO

When you want to perform the macro again, pull down the Tools menu and click on Macro to see the Macro dialog box (Figure 10.2). Double-click on the name of the macro in the list, or click on the macro and click on Run.

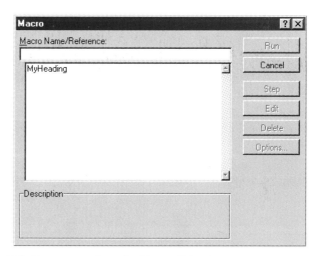

**Figure 10.2** Run a macro from the Macro dialog box

**CAUTION**

*If you assign an uppercase letter to a macro, remember to hold down CTRL and SHIFT when you press the letter to run the macro.*

# ASSIGNING MACROS TO KEYSTROKES AND MENUS

It's easy to run a macro by selecting it in the Macro dialog box, but it would even be easier if you could just press a shortcut key combination or choose the macro from a menu. You can choose either or both of these options, using the expanded Record New Macro dialog box.

Look again at the expanded dialog box in Figure 10.1. If you want to assign the macro to the Tools menu, click on the Menu Item on Tools Menu checkbox, and then type the prompt you want to appear on the menu in the text box. After you record the macro, that text will appear when you pull down the Tools menu—just click on it to run the macro. Just remember that the macro will only appear in the Tools menu when the workbook containing the macro is open (unless, of course, the macro is stored in the Personal.xls workbook).

You can also assign the macro to a shortcut key combination with the CTRL key. To do this, click on the Shortcut Key checkbox, then enter the letter in the box next to Ctrl+. For each macro that you assign a combination to, Excel changes the letter—e, j, k, l, m, q, and t, followed by the uppercase letters A through Z—skipping over those lowercase letters already used by Excel, such as Ctrl+i for italic.

You can assign to a macro a letter already used by Excel. Pressing the combination will run your macro, not the Excel command. To return the shortcut key combination to its original purpose, you have to delete the macro—a subject I'll cover a little later.

## upgrade note

*If you've created macros with versions of Excel prior to version 5 for Windows, then you're probably familiar with the Excel Macro language. To record a macro in that language, rather than in Visual Basic, click on the MS Excel 4.0 Macro option in the Language section of the Record New Macro dialog box.*

# Assigning an Existing Macro

I can hear you—"So now you tell me how to do that." Stay cool. You can assign a macro a shortcut key or assign it to the Tools menu even if you've already recorded it. Open the worksheet where you've stored the macro (if it's not in the Personal Macro Workbook), then choose Macro from the Tools menu to see a list of the available macros. Click on the macro that you want to assign, and then click on Options to see the Macro Options dialog box shown in Figure 10.3.

Use the Assign to section to add the macro to the Tools menu or to assign it a key combination, just as you can when you're recording a macro.

The Help Information section, by the way, is pretty interesting because it lets you create your own help system for the macros that you assign to the Tools menu. I wouldn't bother tackling the section if I were you, unless you want to devote a lot of time to learning macros, but the Status Bar Text option is useful. Whatever you type in that text box will appear in the status bar when you point to the macro item in the Tools menu or to a toolbar button (see the next section).

**Figure 10.3**  Macro Options for an existing macro

# ADDING MACROS TO A TOOLBAR

If you create a lot of macros, trying to remember the shortcut key combinations you assigned to each can be a problem. And you can only add so many commands to the Tools menu before it reaches the bottom of the screen. For a macro that you use a lot, assign it to a toolbar button so you can run it with a single click.

There's another great reason to use the toolbar. When you assign a macro to the toolbar, you don't have to open the workbook where the macro is stored yourself. When you click on the button, Excel will open the worksheet for you automatically. You can assign a macro to any of the toolbars you see on the screen.

As an example, let's assign the MyHeading macro to the Standard toolbar. Just follow along. Right-click on any toolbar and then select Customize from the shortcut menu. Scroll through the Categories list and click on Custom to see a list of generic, unassigned buttons.

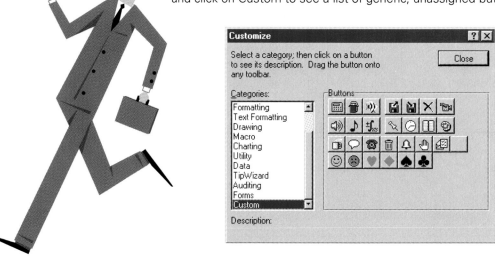

Pick a button that you'd like to assign to the macro, and drag it to the position on the toolbar where you want it to be inserted. When you release the mouse, Excel displays the Assign Macro dialog box listing all of the available macros. Double-click on MyHeading to assign it to the button and then on OK. Finally, close the Customize dialog box. Now whenever you want to insert your heading in a worksheet, just click on the button.

*See Chapter 3 for more about toolbars.*

You can also assign a macro to any of the buttons already on the toolbar. Just remember that changing one of the built-in buttons takes away its default function. To reassign a button, display the Customize dialog box, right-click on the toolbar button that you want to modify and choose Assign Macro from the shortcut menu. Then select the macro from the list and click on OK.

# ASSIGNING A MACRO TO A GRAPHIC OBJECT

Assigning a macro to the toolbar is convenient, but a toolbar can only hold so many buttons. If you have a macro that you run only in a specific worksheet, why take up space in the toolbar? You can still run the macro with a click by assigning it to a graphic object on the worksheet itself.

In Chapter 9, you learned how to draw graphic shapes. You can convert a graphic into a button by assigning a macro to it. To run the macro, just select the object. Because the graphic is saved as part of the worksheet, it is available whenever the worksheet is displayed onscreen. To assign a macro to a graphic, follow the steps shown here.

## Creating Macro Buttons

1. Display the Drawing toolbar and select the graphic object so it is surrounded by handles.
2. Right-click on the object and choose Assign Macro from the shortcut menu.
3. In the dialog box that appears, double-click on the macro that you want to assign to the object.

# DELETING MACROS

It's pretty straightforward to delete a macro—just follow the steps on the next page.

## SHORTCUT

*You can create a macro and assign it to a graphic object in one operation. After choosing Assign Macro from the shortcut menu, click on Record in the dialog box, then record that macro you want to assign.*

## DELETING A MACRO step by step

**1.** Pull down the Tools menu and click on Macro.

**2.** Click on the macro you want to delete.

**3.** Click on Delete.

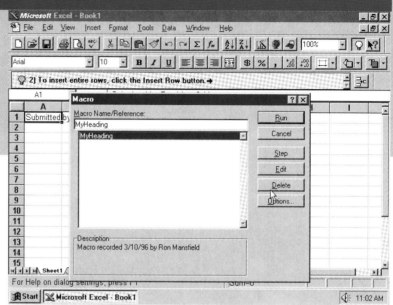

## CAUTION

*If you do not delete the macro from the Tools menu first, you'll have to edit the menu later using the Menu Editor option, which you can only access from an Excel module. It's not something a very busy person should consider.*

To delete a macro from the Personal Macro Workbook, you have to display it first. I'll cover that in a moment. To delete all of the macros from the Personal Macro Workbook, however, just delete the file Personal.xls (stored in the XLStart subfolder in your Excel folder). Don't worry, Excel will create a new personal workbook the next time you choose to save a macro there.

Before you delete a macro, however, stop and think a minute. Have you assigned the macro to the Tools menu? If you did, then you should remove it from the Tools menu *before* you delete it. Otherwise, the macro will be deleted but the command will still appear in the menu. Choose Macro from the Tools menu, click on the macro in the list box, then click on Options. Deselect the Menu Item in Tools Menu checkbox, then select OK.

If you delete a macro that was assigned to a shortcut key combination, you'll see an error message the next time you press the combination. Just ignore the message and click on OK to clear it from the screen. The next time you press the combination you'll just hear a beep, Excel's way of telling you the combination is no longer assigned.

If the deleted macro was assigned to the toolbar, the button will still appear. To remove the button, right-click on a toolbar and select Customize. Then drag the button down off the toolbar—it will be deleted when you release the mouse button. You can then close the dialog box.

# DISPLAYING THE PERSONAL MACRO WORKBOOK

You cannot delete or modify a macro that you've assigned to the Personal Macro Workbook until you unhide it. The workbook is opened when you start Excel, but it does not appear in a window. To display the workbook, pull down the Window menu and click on Unhide. You'll see a dialog box listing all of your hidden windows—there will usually only be one. Click on Personal.xls, then click on OK. The workbook will appear with the codes of the macro displayed in a module page. You can now delete or modify a macro in the Personal Macro Workbook from any workbook that's open.

You can leave the Personal Macro Workbook unhidden, and switch to your other workbook using the Window menu. However, if you exit Excel when the Personal Macro Workbook is unhidden, it will appear onscreen the next time you start Excel. If you close the Personal Macro Workbook when it is unhidden, however, you won't be able to use its macros until you open it again. So, rather than close it, just hide it again. Display the workbook onscreen and then choose Hide from the Window menu.

# LEARNING MORE ABOUT MACROS

Now here's the dilemma. If you're a very busy person, then you can really use macros. But, learning all about macros is like learning another language. I've just touched on the very basics here to get you started.

To learn more about macros, spend some time visiting the Excel Help system. There are plenty of help topics on all phases of macros. If you want to learn more about the inner workings of the macro language, then display the Contents page of the Help system, scroll the list and click on the Microsoft Excel Visual Basic Reference. Most of

*The Excel Visual Basic Reference is not installed by default. You might need to run the Setup program to add this feature. See Appendix A for details.*

**habits & strategies**

*You can learn a lot by recording macros, and then looking at the Visual Basic commands that Excel created for you in the module sheet.*

the information is pretty technical, but it will mean more as you get to know Visual Basic, the language of Excel macros.

If you just want to see what a Visual Basic macro looks like, unhide the Personal Macro Workbook or the module sheet of a workbook that contains its own macros. To display a module, click on the Last Tab button, on the far left of the horizontal scroll bar, to see a tab called Module1. Then click on the Module1 tab. Take a look at the macro to see if you can figure out the commands—the MyHeading macro is shown in Figure 10.4. When you're ready to return to the worksheet, just click on the First Tab button.

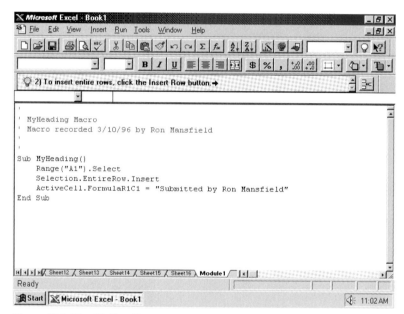

**Figure 10.4** The MyHeading macro in the module sheet

# WHAT NEXT?

In Chapter 11 you'll see how to really automate complex what-if projects by employing the Scenario Manager and Solver.

CAFÉ

MAIL

# Automating
# What-If Projects

- Organizing what-if projects

- Using scenarios

- Finding the right number with Solver

# FAST FORWARD

## CREATE A SCENARIO ➤ *pp 214-216*

1. Design your what-if worksheet.
2. Select the changing cells in the worksheet.
3. Select Scenarios from the Tools menu.
4. Click on Add.
5. Type the scenario name.
6. Drag over the contents of the Changing Cells text box.
7. Select a protection option, if desired.
8. Click on OK.
9. Enter the changing cell values.
10. Click on Add.
11. Repeat steps 4 through 10 for each scenario, then click on OK.

## VIEW SCENARIOS ➤ *p 217*

1. Select Scenarios from the Tools menu.
2. Click on the scenario name you want to display.
3. Click on Show.

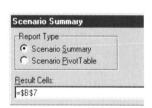

## CREATE A SCENARIO SUMMARY ➤ *p 217*

1. Select Scenarios from the Tools menu.
2. Click on Summary.
3. Enter or select the Result Cells.
4. Select the Report Type: Scenario Summary or Scenario PivotTable.
5. Click on OK.

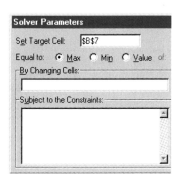

## CHANGE A SCENARIO ➤ *p 218*

1. Select Scenarios from the Tools menu.
2. Click on the scenario name you want to change.
3. Click on Edit.
4. Make desired changes to the name, changing cells, and protection.
5. Click on OK.
6. Make the desired changes to the changing cell values.
7. Click on OK.

## USE SOLVER ➤ *pp 219-224*

1. Create the what-if project.
2. Click on the target cell.
3. Pull down the Tools menu and click on Solver.
4. Choose Max, Min, or Value and enter a specific value.
5. Enter or drag over the changing cells or click on Guess.
6. Click on Add to add a constraint.
7. Enter or click on the cell reference.
8. Select an operator.
9. Enter the Constraint value.
10. Click on Add.
11. Repeat steps 7 through 10 for each constraint.
12. Click on Close.
13. Click on Solve.
14. Choose to keep the results that Solver found, or restore the original values.
15. If you want to save the scenario, click on Save Scenario, enter a scenario name, and then click on OK.
16. Select one or more report types.
17. Click on OK.

It was the first successful electronic spreadsheet—Visi-Calc, actually—that first brought the PC to the attention of the business world. What really triggered our imaginations, I suspect, was its ability to solve *what-if* problems. As soon as we realized how easy it was to get answers, however, we had more questions. This often meant solving the same problem over and over and over again with just a slight twist. "What if we raised the rate to 10.2%, or 10.3%, or 10.4%?" "How much would the building cost if we built it in Colorado or West Virginia or on Maui?" Naturally, you can manually enter and re-enter variables like these and see or print the results yourself. But there is a better way. You can give Excel the *parameters* for various *scenarios* and have the answers computed automatically. And isn't that what personal computing is all about—eliminating grunt work, not creating more work for us? In this chapter, you'll learn ways to finish your what-if chores in a hurry.

# GENERAL ORGANIZATIONAL TIPS

Answering a what-if problem is a snap if you take your time and plan ahead. The most common problem that people have is remembering to design the worksheet so it includes all of the proper variables.

Locating the variables and answer cells cleverly can save you time and frustration too. The answer to your what-if problem will be values in one or more cells. These are called *result* or *target* cells, and they must contain formulas or functions that reference the changing cells. If you place

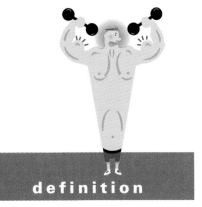

*Variables: The cells that you change to see what happens if you change them, sometimes called the "changing cells."*

*Strategically grouping variables
and answer cells can make your
life easier. (You'll see examples
of this throughout the chapter.)
Keep the worksheet simple.
This will make it easier to
change values, see results,
and select cells.*

these close to the changing cells, you'll have to spend less time scrolling around the worksheet to see your results.

Look at your what-if worksheet carefully. Make certain that you've included all of the variables—the changing cells—that affect the results. And make sure that there aren't any stray cell references in formulas or functions that can affect the results without your being aware.

# USING SCENARIO MANAGER

One of the problems with what-if problems is that you have to change the variable cells to see the effect on the entire worksheet. You make a change, look at the sheet, make another change and look at it again. If you have a number of variable cells, it is difficult to keep track of which ones you've changed and the effect on the worksheet. You could print out a copy of each sheet after changing the variables, or you could make a list of the results on paper. But doesn't that sort of fly in the face of this wonderful technology that Excel gives us?

Enter Scenario Manager. Scenario Manager lets you "capture" each what-if result. It saves each combination of the variable cells as a scenario, so you can quickly see the result of each scenario by just selecting it from a list. But in addition, you can generate a report summarizing all of the scenarios. Print out a copy of the report and analyze your what-if problem at your leisure.

To create a scenario, you'll need a worksheet containing your what-if problem. As an example, let's use the simple mortgage analyzer shown here:

| | A | B | C |
|---|---|---|---|
| 1 | | | |
| 2 | | | |
| 3 | Income | 85000 | |
| 4 | Loan Amount | 125,000 | |
| 5 | Interest Rate | 9.2% | |
| 6 | Term | 30 | |
| 7 | Payment | 1023.818 | |
| 8 | | | |
| 9 | Total Paid | 368574.6 | |
| 10 | | | |

*The formula to calculate the monthly mortgage payment in cell B7 is =PMT(B5/12,B6\*12,-B4). The formula to calculate the total amount paid in cell B9 is =(B6\*12\*B7).*

To perform a what-if analysis, you would change the values in cells B4, B5, or B6. What if the interest rate goes down to 8%, or you take out a 15-year loan, or borrow less money? How will that affect your monthly mortgage payment and the amount that you pay? There are an awful lot of combinations that you can try, too many to trust your memory. So rather than even try to, create a set of scenarios.

Each scenario will include a different combination of values in the changing cells. One scenario will look at the maximum monthly payment, another will look at the minimum, and another will look at the values that you'd prefer for your mortgage. We'll be creating only three scenarios, but you can have as many as you need for your own what-if problems.

## Creating a Scenario

To create a scenario, first make sure you understand which cells you want to change, although you don't have to use the same ones with every scenario. In this case, we'll be using the same cells for all three scenarios—cells B4, B5, and B6.

Select Scenarios from the Tools menu to see the dialog box shown in Figure 11.1. This is the box that will later list the individual scenarios you can choose from to see the results on the worksheet. Right now, nothing is listed because you haven't yet created a scenario.

**SHORTCUT**

*Enter the what-if values and select the changing cells before starting to create the first scenario—the values will automatically be used in the Scenario Manager dialog box.*

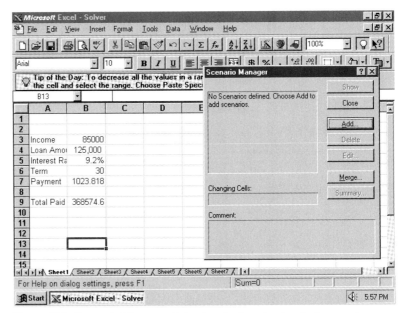

**Figure 11.1** Scenario Manager dialog box for keeping track of scenarios

To create your first scenario, click on Add to see the box shown in Figure 11.2. This is where you name the scenario, so you can refer to it later, and where you choose which cells you want to change. First, enter a name for the scenario that explains how it fits into the scheme of things. For example, I'd enter Maximum, because this first scenario assumes the maximum monthly payment—the largest loan, the highest interest, the shortest loan period.

*To select non-consecutive changing cells, click on the first, then hold down CTRL while you click on the remaining ones.*

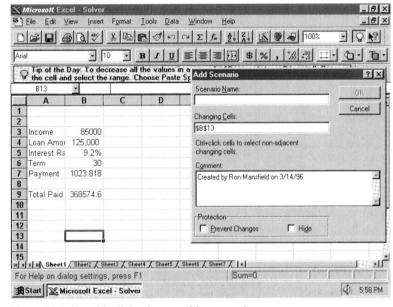

**Figure 11.2**  Use this dialog box to add a scenario

## habits & strategies

*When you're busy, you may have a tendency to ignore entering a description, as I'm doing here. It is usually worth the few seconds it takes to enter a brief description explaining the particular combinations of values that will make up the scenario.*

The current active or selected cells will be listed in the Changing Cells box. Drag the dialog box out of the way, so you can see which cells you want to change as part of the scenario. Drag over the contents of the text box (so they will be deleted when you select other cells), and then drag over the changing cells B4, B5, and B6 in the worksheet.

Next, consider if you want to use protection. Prevent Changes means that no one will be able to change the scenario. Hide means it will not be listed in the list of scenarios. To actually implement either choice, however, you must protect the worksheet itself. I'll discuss that later.

Click on OK. You'll see a dialog box showing the changing cells and their current contents:

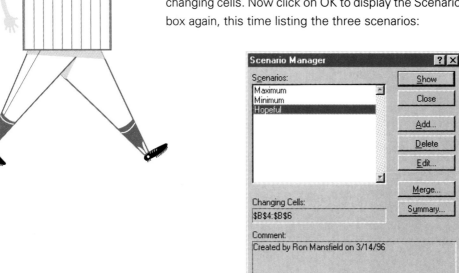

If you already entered the values for the scenario, just click on OK to save it. Otherwise, enter the values that you'd like to apply in the text boxes now. If you've entered the worksheet as I've shown, leave the values as they are and then click on Add to create another scenario. The Add Scenario box appears, so you can name a new scenario, select other changing cells (if you want to), and pick protection options. Type **Minimum** as the next scenario name, and then click on OK.

Now let's change the values in the changing cells to create another scenario. For cell B4, enter **75000**, for cell B5 enter **.05**, and for cell B6 enter **35**, and then click on Add for one more scenario. Name it Hopeful, click on OK, and then enter **80000**, **0.06**, and **25** in the three changing cells. Now click on OK to display the Scenario Manager dialog box again, this time listing the three scenarios:

# Viewing Scenarios

Scenarios are saved along with the worksheet. Whenever you want to see how the changing cells affect the results, select Scenarios from the Tools menu. The Scenario Manager dialog box will appear listing the scenarios that you created. Drag the box out of the way so you can see the result cells (in this example, cells B7 and B9). Click on the scenario you want to see and click on the Show button. Each time you do, Excel changes the values in the changing cells to match those entered in the scenario, so you can see their effects immediately.

When you're done, click on Close. The worksheet will display the values from the last scenario viewed.

# Scenario Summaries

It is easy to change to different scenarios, but that doesn't make it any easier to remember the results later on. By creating a summary report, you can compare the changing cells and the results side-by-side in a separate worksheet. To create a report, click on Summary in the Scenario Manager to see a dialog box like this:

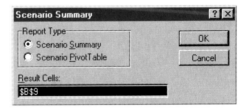

You can create two types of summary reports. First, however, drag or click on the cells which display the results to display those cell references in the Result Cells text box. For example, in the mortgage analysis, I'd click on cell B7, the monthly payment, and then CTRL-click on cell B9, the total paid. This way, the report will show the results of changing variables on those two cells.

To create a report, click on Summary Report and then on OK. Excel will create a new worksheet and display the summary as shown in Figure 11.3. It shows the values applied by each scenario and the resulting values. By printing this out, you have a recap of each combination in the what-if analysis.

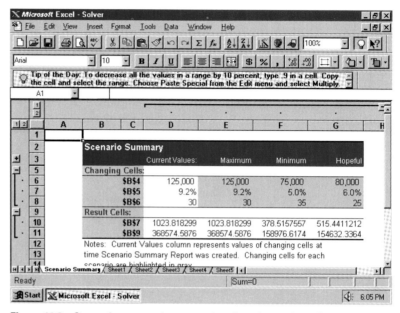

Figure 11.3 shown with:

| | | Current Values: | Maximum | Minimum | Hopeful |
|---|---|---|---|---|---|
| **Scenario Summary** | | | | | |
| **Changing Cells:** | | | | | |
| | $B$4 | 125,000 | 125,000 | 75,000 | 80,000 |
| | $B$5 | 9.2% | 9.2% | 5.0% | 6.0% |
| | $B$6 | 30 | 30 | 35 | 25 |
| **Result Cells:** | | | | | |
| | $B$7 | 1023.818299 | 1023.818299 | 378.5157557 | 515.4411212 |
| | $B$9 | 368574.5876 | 368574.5876 | 158976.6174 | 154632.3364 |

Notes: Current Values column represents values of changing cells at time Scenario Summary Report was created. Changing cells for each scenario are highlighted in gray.

**Figure 11.3** Scenario summaries recap the changing and result cells of a what-if problem

*With Scenario Manager you can also delete scenarios and merge—or copy—scenarios from other worksheets.*

**CAUTION**

*You can enter a password if you want, but don't forget it. You may not be able to change your worksheet without it.*

# Changing Scenarios

If you want to see other combinations of variables, create additional scenarios. You can also change existing scenarios to modify the name, the changing cells, and the values of the variable.

Click on the scenario name in Scenario Manager and then on Edit to see the Edit Scenario box—an almost identical twin to the Add Scenario box. Edit the name, changing cells, description, and protection, then click on OK to display the values. When the values are correct, click on OK—there is no Add option this time around.

# Protecting the Scenarios

Choosing a protection option in the Add or Edit Scenario boxes does not do the job completely. To implement the option, you have to protect the worksheet. After closing the Scenario Manager, pull down the Tools menu, point to Protection, and then click on Protect Sheet to see the following dialog box.

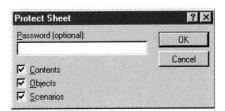

*You can add scenarios when the worksheet is protected, but you won't be able to edit or delete them—those two buttons will be dimmed. To edit or delete scenarios you must unprotect the worksheet—pull down the Tools menu, point to Protection, and click on Unprotect sheet.*

Select the Scenarios checkbox, if it is not already selected, and then click on OK.

# FINDING THE RIGHT NUMBER WITH SOLVER

Scenario Manager makes things easier, but what if you're looking for a specific result? You know the result you want to achieve, but not the combination of variables. For example, suppose you want to pay $850 per month on a mortgage. How many combinations of loan amounts, interest rates, and terms would you have to enter to yield that payment amount? Do you have the time to add scenarios for every possible value, watching the result cells to see which gives you the answer you want? No way. Instead, you can have Excel find the values for you using *Solver*. Solver will continually apply values to changing cells until a result cell reaches the maximum, minimum, or specific value that you designate.

## Loading Solver

Solver is an extra feature of Excel that is added to the basic core of Excel features. Because many people won't use it, Solver is part of a group of similar features called add-ins. It takes some time, and memory, to load the add-ins into Excel, so you can choose which of them you want to use.

If Solver is not listed in your Tools menu, then it was not one of the add-ins loaded when you started Excel. To install Solver—or any other add-in feature—pull down the Tools menu and click on Add-Ins to see the following dialog box.

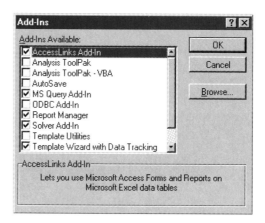

Scroll the list and select the checkbox for Solver Add-In, and for any other features that you want to add. You can also deselect those you don't want to bother loading. Then select OK. Excel will load the add-ins that you selected; you do not have to wait until the next time you start Excel.

## Solving What-If Problems

**habits & strategies**

*To make Excel run faster, deselect Add-Ins you do not plan on using.*

When you want to solve a problem, first create a what-if worksheet. As an example, I'll use the same mortgage analysis worksheet that we used for scenarios. This time, we'll let Solver change the values for us.

Click on the cell that you want to find the value for, called the *target cell* in Solver—in this case, cell B7. The cell must contain a formula or function that is calculated from other cells in the worksheet. Next, pull down the Tools menu and click on Solver to see this dialog box:

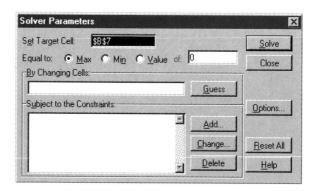

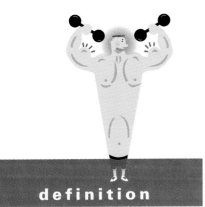

The address of the target cell will appear in the Set Target Cell box. If it is not the cell you want to calculate, drag the dialog box out of the way and click on the target cell in the worksheet.

Next, choose the result you want Solver to calculate—the maximum or minimum calculated value, or a specific value. For example, if you were trying to find a combination of variables that will give you a monthly payment of $850, click on Value and enter **850** in the text box.

The next step is to designate the changing cells—the cells you want Solver to modify to arrive at the result. You could enter the cells yourself into the By Changing Cells box, but instead click on Guess. Excel examines the target cell, identifying the cell references in the formula or function, and then automatically assigns them as the changing cells. If the guess is incorrect, change them yourself.

So far so good. But there is one problem. Depending on your worksheet, there may be many combinations of variables that achieve the same result. In most instances, you aren't just interested in the result, but how you get there. For example, Solver could possibly calculate an $850 monthly mortgage payment based on a 1% loan. Since it's highly unlikely that you'll find such a loan—unless it's from a very close relative—the solution is invalid. You need to set some ground rules under which Solver will work, called constraints.

Constraints tell Solver the realities of life. In our mortgage example, we'll use a few simple constraints:

- The mortgage amount must be at least $80,000 but no more than four times your annual salary.
- The interest rate must be at least 6% but no more than 10%.
- The length of the loan must be for less than 31 years.

All of your constraints will be listed in the Subject to the Constraints list, and you use the Add, Change, and Delete buttons to work with them. Click on Add now to create the first constraint, displaying this dialog box:

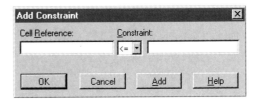

*Constraint types are >=, =, <=, and Int.*
*Int requires an integer value.*

# CAUTION

*If you choose Add and*
*decide not to create another*
*constraint, click on Close.*
*You'll get an error message*
*if you click on OK.*

There are three sections to the box—the Cell Reference, the Constraint operator, and the Constraint value. The Cell Reference is the address of a changing cell, the Constraint operator is a logical operator, and the Constraint value is a value or cell reference limiting the changing cell.

A constraint is in the form of a formula that evaluates to either a true or false value, and it can test for only one value. The limitations on the valid mortgage amount must be formed by two constraints. The first will limit the amount to at least $80,000, the second to no more than four times the annual income.

The insertion point should be in the Cell Reference box, so click on cell B4. Excel will insert $B$4 into the box. Pull down the arrow to see the list for the operators and select >=. Next, click in the Constraint text box and type **80000**.

Now click on Add to accept the constraint and to create the next one. Click on B4 again as the cell reference, choose the <= operator, and enter **4*B3** in the Constraint text box. Click on OK to accept the constraint and to redisplay the Solver Parameters dialog box listing the two constraints.

Now on your own add the following additional constraints:

- B5 <= **0.1**
- B5 >= **0.06**
- B6 <= **30**

They should appear in the dialog box like this:

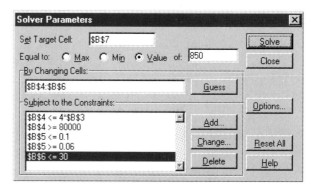

When you're done, display the Solver Parameters dialog box, and click on Solve. Solver will begin applying values to the changing cells, keeping within the limitations of the constraints, and observing the target cell. When it finds a combination, it shows the results in the worksheet, along with this dialog box:

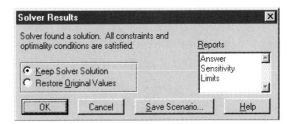

Choose whether you want to keep the results that Solver found, or restore the original values. If you click on Save Scenario, you can enter a scenario name, and Excel will save the values of the changing cells as a scenario. You can then choose to restore the original values, but quickly display the Solver solution by viewing the scenario from Scenario Manager.

You can also select to create three types of reports. To generate a report, click on each type you want and then on OK. Excel creates the report(s) in another worksheet or worksheets. An Answer report shows the original and final values of the target cell and the changing cells, along with the constraints. A Sensitivity report explains how sensitive the solution is to small changes in the target cell formula or in the constraints. A Limits report shows the values, and the lower and upper limits of the target and changing cells while satisfying the constraints.

## Solver Options

While it is easy to use Solver, it is really a very complex and sophisticated tool. To get some idea how Solver works, display the Solver dialog box and click on Options to see the box shown in Figure 11.4.

If you feel at home with terms such as Quadratic Extrapolation and Linear Module, then you'll have no trouble understanding what this is all about. There are a few options, however, that are still useful for the rest of us.

The Max Time setting, for example, determines how long Solver can take to find a result. The default is 100 seconds; you can have it go as long as 32,767 seconds (about 546 minutes). Iterations control how many times Solver substitutes values for the changing cells—the number of run-throughs.

### SHORTCUT

*You can click on multiple report types and Excel will automatically create each specified type one after the other.*

*If you don't like the solution that Solver found, modify the constraints and try it again. To modify a constraint, click on it in the Solver Parameters box and click on Change.*

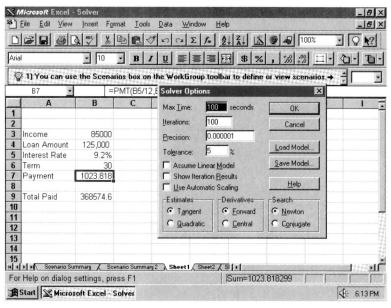

**Figure 11.4**  Use Solver Options to customize how it works

You use the Save Model and Load Model options to save (and later reuse) the Solver parameters. Select Save Model to store the problem on a disk, and select Load Model when you want to run the Solver again.

## Learning More About Solver

Solver is more than a great time-saver. It is, as its name implies, a problem-solver. As you work more with what-if problems, you'll find more instances when Solver can come to the rescue.

To learn more about Solver, use the Help system and the sample files provided with Excel in the Excel\Examples\Solver folder. You'll find examples of Solver features in the Solverex.xls workbook, and types of problems that Solver can solve in the Solvsamp.xls workbook. Solvsamp includes six worksheets containing typical business what-if problems.

*The Excel folder might be in your Microsoft Office folder.*

Display the worksheet you want to use, pull down the Tools menu and click on Solver. The parameters will already be set. Try to determine how the worksheet operates, and how the parameters and other constraints have been applied, then click on Solve to see the solution.

## WHAT'S NEXT?

Next step—auditing and troubleshooting. We're almost done!

PRIORITY!

# Auditing and Troubleshooting

# FAST FORWARD

## INTERPRET ERROR VALUES ➤ *pp 230-233*

Error values (messages) appear both in the cell containing the flawed formula and in cells adversely affected:

- #DIV/0! stands for division by zero.
- #N/A means no value available.
- #NAME? is displayed when you've improperly referred to a named item.
- #NULL! means that you've referred to two non-intersecting areas.
- #NUM! appears when there are unacceptable numeric arguments in formulas or when a formula can't reach a workable result.
- #REF! indicates a missing reference point (perhaps after deleting a cell used by a formula).
- #VALUE! reminds you that you've used the wrong kind of argument, value, or operand.

## OPEN THE AUDITING TOOLBAR ➤ *p 233*

1. Make certain no cells are hidden in the sheet or workbook to be audited.
2. Right-click anywhere on a toolbar.
3. Choose Auditing from the shortcut menu.
4. A floating toolbar appears.
5. Move or dock it if you like.

## SEE CELLS PROVIDING DATA FOR A FORMULA ➤ *pp 234-235*

1. Make certain no cells are hidden in the sheet or workbook to be audited.
2. Select the cell containing the formula of interest.
3. Click the Trace Precedents button in the Auditing toolbar once to see an arrow indicating the first contributing (precedent) cell.
4. Click the Trace Precedents button multiple times to see additional contributing cells.
5. Blue arrows appear with blue dots in each cell affecting the formula. Red arrows indicate some (but not all) types of errors.

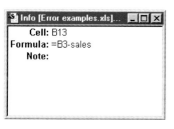

| 3 | Ticket sales | $ 247,478 | |
| 4 | | | |
| 5 | Boat costs | $ 43,589 | 21% |
| 6 | Labor costs | $ 89,102 | 42% |
| 7 | Advertising costs | $ 27,500 | 13% |
| 8 | Insurance costs | $ 24,892 | 12% |
| 9 | Office costs | $ 14,875 | 7% |
| 10 | Misc. costs | $ 12,222 | 6% |
| 11 | Totals | $ 212,180 | 100% |
| 12 | Profit | $ 35,298 | |

## SEE WHICH FORMULAS
## USE DATA IN A CELL ➤ *p 235*

1. Make certain no cells are hidden in the sheet or workbook to be audited.
2. Select the cell containing the value of interest.
3. Click the Trace Dependents button in the Auditing toolbar once to see an arrow indicating the first (dependent) cell containing a formula using the data.
4. Click the Trace Dependents button multiple times to see additional cells.
5. Blue arrows appear with blue dots in each cell affected by the active cell. Red arrows indicate some (but not all) types of errors.
6. Double-click an arrow to select the cell at the other end of the line.

Info [Error examples.xls]...

**Cell:** B13
**Formula:** =B3-sales
**Note:**

## USE INFO WINDOWS IN CELLS ➤ *pp 236-237*

1. Select the cell of interest.
2. Click the Show Info Window button in the Auditing toolbar.
3. A window appears showing the cell location, the formula, and notes, if any.
4. Use the Info command on the resulting menu bar to choose other Info options (Names, Protection, etc.).
5. Choose other cells of interest and read about them in the Info window or use the Close box to close the window.

☑ Iteration
Maximum Iterations: 100
Maximum Change: 0.001

## USE ITERATIONS FOR
## CIRCULAR REFERENCES ➤ *pp 238-239*

1. Select the cell containing the circular reference.
2. Choose Options from the Tools menu.
3. Bring the Calculation tab forward.
4. Place a check in the Iteration box, and specify the maximum number of iterations and the maximum change amount.
5. Press F9 to view the results without closing the dialog box and make changes in your settings if necessary.
6. Click OK to close the Options dialog box.

**T**here are three kinds of errors: those you find, those someone else finds, and those nobody finds. I don't know which kind is the worst. They can all be expensive and time-consuming.

Excel provides a number of devices designed to help you locate and eliminate common errors. These include *Error values*, the *Info window*, and the *Auditing toolbar*. To help you cope with problems created by circular references, this chapter discusses these tools and the Iteration feature.

## USE YOUR HEAD

Before we explore *automated* troubleshooting, it is worth mentioning that you can find a lot of problems on your own. Look at the worksheet. Do the results sound reasonable? Try using your worksheet to run multiple examples drawn from as familiar a set of data as you have available. If you have the luxury of setting things aside for a day or two, do that and revisit the new worksheet when you are fresh.

## USING ERROR VALUES TO LOCATE PROBLEMS

Some problems present themselves to you right when you finish a worksheet (or even while you are creating it). Frequently, problems manifest themselves as *error values* (messages) in one or more cells. There are seven error values. They always start with the pound sign (#):

- #DIV/0!
- #N/A
- #NAME?
- #NULL!
- #NUM!
- #REF!
- #VALUE!

These values appear both in cells *containing* erroneous formulas and in cells with formulas that *refer* to the erroneous formulas. Thus, you may need to inspect more than one cell to find the real source of

## CAUTION

*Just because your worksheet is error-free when you complete it, that does not mean it will automatically stay that way. Protect cells containing formulas as detailed in Chapter 1. Make backups of tested worksheets.*

the problem. Although they should never be *completely* ignored, error values like these sometimes appear simply because you are not finished creating the worksheet. For instance, if you create a formula that performs division using the contents of a cell as the divisor, and if that referenced cell is empty because you haven't entered a value into it yet, you'll see Excel's #DIV/0! value. The error value should disappear when you place an appropriate divisor in the referenced cell.

Let's look at each of the error values and consider what they mean and what to do when you see them.

# #DIV/0!

You'll see this error when Excel tries to divide by zero, or if a referenced cell is blank when it needs to contain a divisor. Some Excel functions return the value of zero under certain circumstances. If your division formula looks to a cell containing a function for a divisor, then the function itself, or one of its arguments, may be causing the problem. Fix the formula if it is referring to the wrong cell, or fix the data in the cell being referenced, or the erroneous function or argument.

# #N/A

N/A means "no value is available." Under certain circumstances, Excel inserts this error value in cells (when you've improperly used certain function arguments, for instance). Other times, you may want to type **#N/A** into cells yourself as a reminder that you need to obtain and enter missing data. Suppose, for instance, that you were creating a worksheet that computes sales commissions for many salespeople and that the commission percentages were still being negotiated for some of them. You could enter **#N/A** as the commission percentages for the "problem" reps. Then, any formulas that rely upon those missing percentages will display #N/A. The #N/A will "ripple through" the rest of your worksheet and be seen in any cell that can't be computed properly without the missing data (totals and subtotals of sales commissions, for example).

# #NAME?

The #NAME? error message usually appears because you've referred to a *named item* improperly. For instance, if you define a cell name or range called Voltage and create a formula like =SQRT(Volts), you'll get the #NAME? error message. (Unless, of course, you also have an item named Volts in your worksheet, in which case Excel will attempt to find the square root of *it*.)

If you name an item, then delete or change its name, you will also get the #NAME? message. Solution: Either rename the item or fix the affected formulas.

You might also see #NAME? if you enter a *function's* name improperly. For instance, the formula =SQR(9) will produce a name error. (The correct function name is SQRT.)

Forgetting to place a colon between cell addresses in a cell range will make Excel think you are referring to a name rather than a range. For example, =SUM(B1B3) will make Excel think you meant an item named B1B3 instead of the range B1:B3.

# #NULL!

The #NULL! message means that you've specified the intersection of two areas that don't intersect, usually in a range specifier. For example, the formula =SUM(A1:D1 A3:D3) produces a null error. Use a comma to separate referenced areas that don't intersect. For instance, =SUM(A1:D1,A3:D3) is permitted.

# #NUM!

You will see the #NUM! error value for several reasons, such as unacceptable numeric arguments in functions. For instance, trying to find the square root of negative numbers will produce the #NUM! error value.

When worksheet functions that use iterations to solve problems can't reach a workable result, you will also see the #NUM! error value. See the section "Using Iteration to Solve Circular References" later in this chapter to learn more about iteration.

# #REF!

The #REF! message is commonly seen after you delete something to which other formulas refer. For instance, if you delete rows or columns containing things that remaining formulas need, you'll see the #REF! value in all affected formulas. Either use Undo to restore the deleted items or fix the formulas.

*Errors can be particularly*

*elusive in large worksheets.*

*Remember to double-check your*

*work, and don't forget to expand*

*outlined worksheets and unhide*

*cells when auditing. You can*

*also use Excel's Auditing toolbar*

*to help you. Among other things,*

*it can show you which cells are*

*used by other cells.*

# #VALUE!

You'll get a value reminder whenever you use the wrong type of argument, value, or operand. For instance, if you have a cell named Sales and you type the formula **="Sales"\*2**, Excel will see the quotation marks and treat sales as text rather than as a name.

Sometimes, however, Excel will convert text automatically. For instance, if you make the cell entry **'10.5** (notice the leading apostrophe) in cell A1, the entry will be formatted and entered as text. You can tell this because it will be left-justified. If you then type the formula **=A1/2** in another cell, Excel will continue to display and treat cell A1 as text, but will convert it to a number for purposes of the formula. Thus, the formula will return the answer 5.25.

# USING THE AUDITING TOOLBAR

The Auditing toolbar, shown in Figure 12.1, can find all of the cells referenced by your fomulas—including the ones in other worksheets.

To display the Auditing toolbar:

1. Right-click anywhere on any Excel toolbar and choose Auditing from the resulting shortcut menu.
2. Drag the toolbar to an out-of-the-way spot, or drag it to an edge of the Excel window to "dock" it. You can also reshape it by dragging on an edge.
3. If you forget the name of a button's function, hover the mouse pointer over the button.

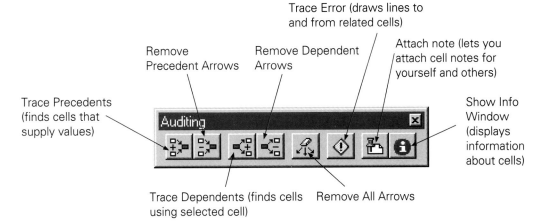

**Figure 12.1** The Auditing toolbar

*The Auditing command on the Tools menu offers a submenu with choices identical to those in the Auditing toolbar. I prefer the toolbar, myself.*

# Tracing Precedents

It is often important to determine which cells contain values or formulas that affect a formula. For example, if a formula computes percentages of two numbers, which two numbers are used, and how were those numbers derived? Were the numbers the result of some other formula?

The Trace Precedents button on the Auditing toolbar (or the equivalent command on the Auditing submenu in the Tools menu) helps you see which cells contribute to a formula. In general, to trace precedents:

1. Expand outlined worksheets and unhide any hidden cells.
2. Click to select the cell containing the formula being audited.
3. Click the Trace Precedents button once to see the first cell or cells contributing to the results in the cell of interest. For example, cells B6 and B11 contribute to C6:

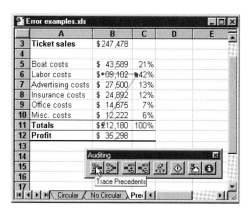

4. To look "farther upstream," to see earlier contributors to the answer, click the Trace Precedents button repeatedly. Here you can tell that one of the numbers used in the percentage computation is the sum of multiple cells:

| | A | B | C |
|---|---|---|---|
| 5 | Boat costs | $ 43,589 | 21% |
| 6 | Labor costs | $ 89,102 | 42% |
| 7 | Advertising costs | $ 27,500 | 13% |
| 8 | Insurance costs | $ 24,892 | 12% |
| 9 | Office costs | $ 14,875 | 7% |
| 10 | Misc. costs | $ 12,222 | 6% |
| 11 | Totals | $ 212,180 | 100% |
| 12 | Profit | $ 35,298 | |

Eventually, you will reach a point where all of the precedents have been displayed. Clicking thereafter will not change the display. To see how to remove arrows, keep reading.

# Tracing Dependents

Values in a worksheet are often used in a variety of formulas. To see which formulas use the data in a cell, follow these steps:

1. Expand outlined worksheets and unhide any hidden cells.
2. Click to select the cell containing the data of interest.
3. Click the Trace Dependents button once to see the first formula using the data. For example, the first click will reveal arrows between cells B5 to B11 and to C5 through C11, since all of these cells use the data in B5. Second and subsequent clicks will reveal indirect relationships, if any:

| 5 | Boat costs | $ 43,509 | 21% |
| 6 | Labor costs | $ 89,102 | 42% |
| 7 | Advertising costs | $ 27,500 | 13% |
| 8 | Insurance costs | $ 24,892 | 12% |
| 9 | Office costs | $ 14,875 | 7% |
| 10 | Misc. costs | $ 12,222 | 6% |
| 11 | Totals | $ 212,180 | 100% |
| 12 | Profit | $ 35,298 | |

# Removing Trace Arrows

There are three buttons for removing trace arrows: Remove Precedent Arrows, Remove Dependent Arrows, and Remove All Arrows. Remove All Arrows does what you'd expect. The other two remove arrows a level at a time, in the reverse order that they were added with their corresponding Trace buttons.

# Tracing Error Messages

The Trace Error choice on the Auditing submenu and Auditing toolbar will take you to the worksheet and cell containing the equation responsible for an error message. For instance, if you see an error like #NAME?, choose Trace Error to take you to the offending cell (B11 in the following example).

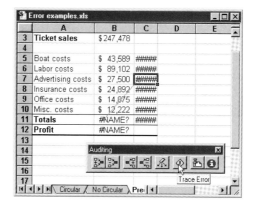

## Attaching Notes

While not strictly a troubleshooting tool, the Attach Notes button appears on the Auditing toolbar, so I will mention it here. I suppose you could use it to make notes to yourself and others about a troublesome cell, so maybe that's why it appears on the toolbar. See Chapter 1 for more about attaching notes.

## Using the Info Window to Find Errors

The Info window gives you another useful troubleshooting tool. It can tell you a lot about the active cell. Here's how to open and use the Info window:

1. Activate the cell of interest.
2. Click the Show Info Window button, or choose Tools|Auditing|Show Info Window.
3. You'll see an Info window containing information about the active cell. Resize and move the window as you would any other.

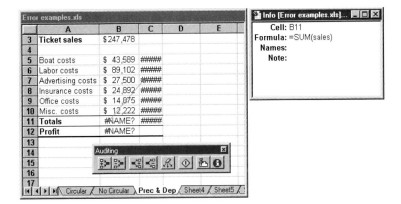

4. As you click from cell to cell, the information changes to reflect the currently active cell.

5. A new menu bar at the top of your screen offers the opportunity to add informational items to the window. Check marks indicate that information will be visible.

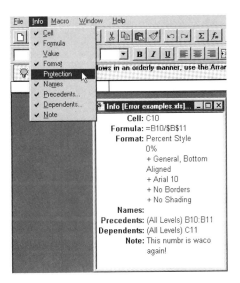

# Printing Info Window Data

When the Info window is active (click in it to make it so), use the File|Print command on the Info Window's menu to print just the window information (and not the worksheet).

# USING ITERATION TO SOLVE CIRCULAR REFERENCES

It is not uncommon to see a dialog box warning that Excel "Cannot resolve circular references." That's not completely true. Excel *can* resolve circular references; you just need to use iteration (multiple passes) to do it. First, here's a review of what a circular reference is. Take a look at this error message.

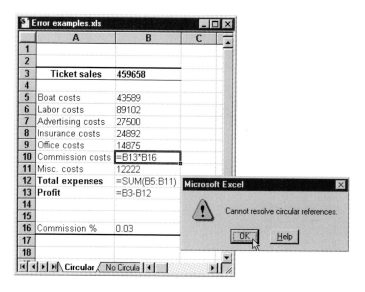

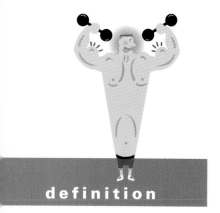

***Circular Reference:*** *A formula in which changes in one or more variables change the results, which affect the variables, which change the result, and on and on, endlessly.*

Suppose you wanted to pay sales commissions based on company profitability, and wished to include commissions as one of the expenses affecting profit. You might create a profit formula in cell B13 that subtracts the expenses (B12) from ticket sales (B3). This would result in a circular reference, since the results of the commission formula in cell B10 will change when expenses change, and expenses will change as commission changes, and so on. The first time you create a formula like this, and each time you load (open) a worksheet containing such a circular reference, you will see a warning.

There are several ways to work around circular reference problems. One way is to redesign the worksheet (and perhaps your commission policy) so that there is a pre-commission profit line, then a commission line, then an actual profit line that takes commissions into consideration. You would pay the sales reps on the pre-commission profit.

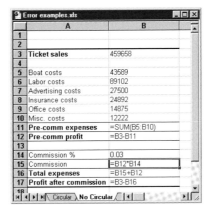

Another approach is to use iteration to resolve the circular reference.

1. Start by selecting the cell containing the circular formula.
2. Choose Options from the Tools menu.
3. Choose the Calculation tab in the Options dialog box.
4. Choose the Iteration check box and specify the Maximum Iterations and the Maximum Change options if you don't like the values shown.

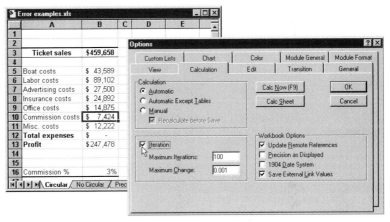

5. Click the Calc Now button or press F9 to see the results. Clicking OK will also run the iteration routine and display an answer in the affected cell(s).

# APPENDIX A

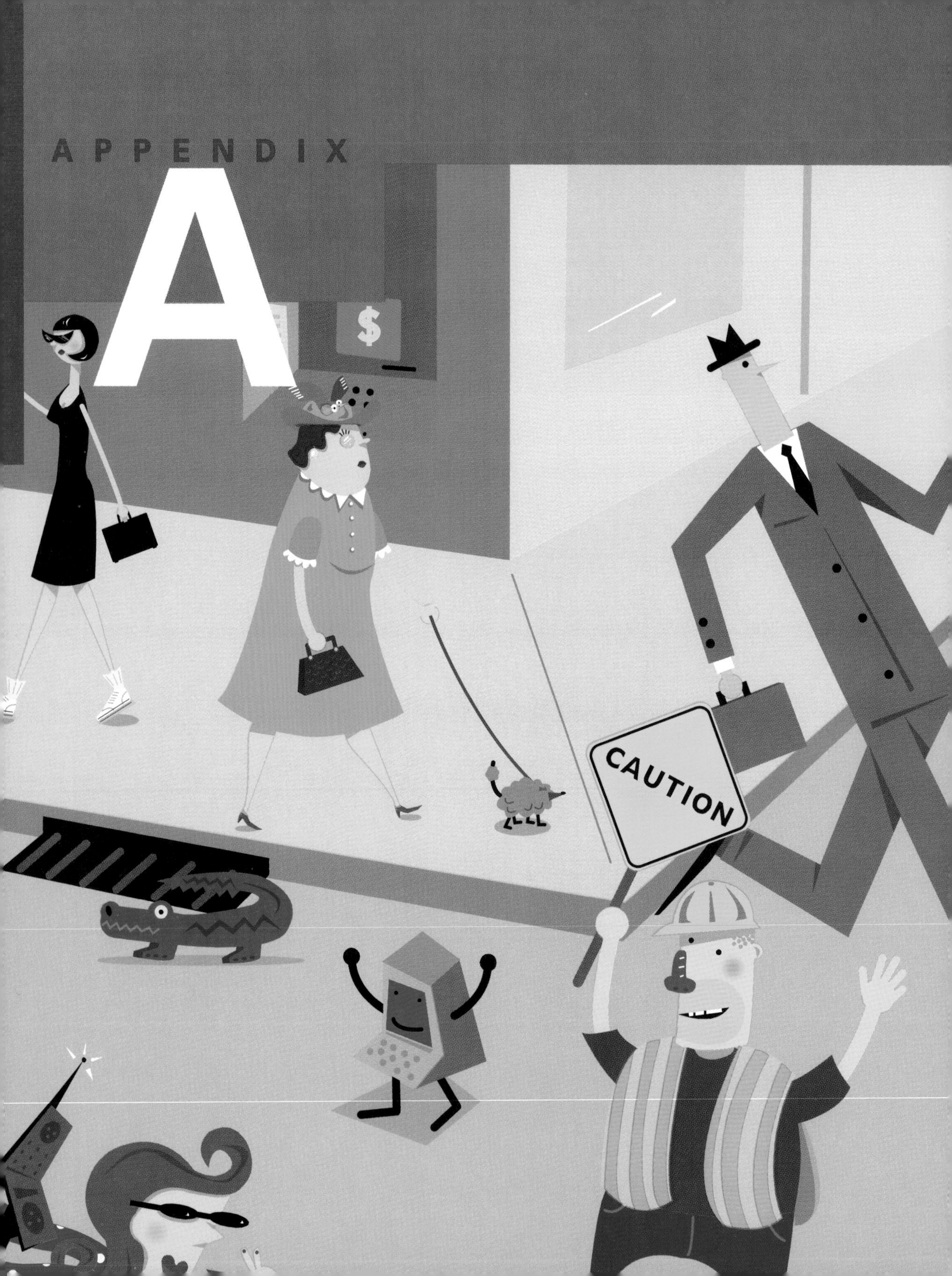

# Installing and Uninstalling Excel

This appendix discusses installing and uninstalling Excel. It also recaps the process of installing and removing Add-ins like the Analysis ToolPac.

# README FILES

Most software manufacturers make last-minute changes and discoveries that are not mentioned in their documentation or online help. Microsoft is no exception. These last-minute items are generally described in text files called *readme files*, or something similar. For example, the initial version of Microsoft Office 95's CD-ROM contains a file called Xlreadme.txt, stored in the Excel folder. Usually you can wait until after you install Excel to read the readme files, but it is possible that information in the files can be helpful before installing.

Sometimes the files are stored on the installation disc or disks as straight text, and all you need to do is double-click to read them. Other times, the readme files are stored in a compressed format, and must be decompressed using the DOS EXTRACT command before you can read them. (For example, if you want to open General.txt, you would type: **a:extract.exe /a /l c:\windows win95_02.cab general.txt**, substituting the drive letter containing the compressed file for a: if necessary.) Frequently, there is at least one non-compressed file that is easy to read, and which lists the filenames of the other readme files.

# STARTING AN EXCEL FOR WINDOWS 95 INSTALLATION FROM A CD-ROM

Here are the general steps for installing Excel from a CD-ROM. Since the exact steps will change based on your system, the product version you've purchased (upgrade, new, Excel only, or Excel as part of Office), be sure to read the screen as you work.

1. Locate your Excel for Windows 95 or Microsoft Office installation CD.
2. Launch Windows 95.
3. Quit all programs that start when you start Windows (virus detectors, the Microsoft Office toolbar, etc.).
4. Choose Run from the Start menu.
5. Type **d:\setup** (substituting a different drive letter for d: if your CD-ROM is not d:).

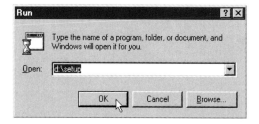

6. Press ENTER or click OK.
7. Skip to the section of this Appendix titled "Completing the Installation."

# STARTING AN EXCEL FOR WINDOWS 95 INSTALLATION FROM FLOPPIES

1. Grab and arrange your Excel for Windows 95 or Microsoft Office installation disks. (I like to place them in numerical order before I start an installation.)
2. Launch Windows 95.
3. Quit all programs that start when you start Windows (virus detectors, the Microsoft Office toolbar, etc.).
4. Choose Run from the Start menu.
5. Type **a:\setup** (substituting a different drive letter for a: if your floppy drive is not a:).

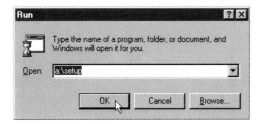

6. Press ENTER or click OK.

# COMPLETING THE INSTALLATION

1. After you've started the installation, the Setup program will perform some routine system checks and inform you of its progress and any problems.
2. If you are installing from floppies, you will be asked repeatedly to insert disks. Be sure the disk you insert is the one you've been asked for. Tapping the ENTER key when the disk is ready will save you a trip to the mouse.
3. When you see the Software License Agreement, scroll through it, reading it thoroughly, checking for typos and loopholes. Click Yes to continue, or write a ten page letter to Microsoft's legal department and purchase Quatro Pro instead.
4. With luck, you'll be greeted by a Setup Wizard whose job it is to lead you through the installation process.
5. Choose the proposed folders (directories) when given choices unless you have some really good reason not to.
6. The Setup program will check for sufficient available disk space, then finish copying files to your hard disk. Floppy users: Pay attention to disk numbers. They are not always requested in ascending, sequential, or numerical order.
7. One day soon you will be rewarded with the Finishing Setup screen. Floppy users: Remember to remove that last floppy!

# ADDING AND REMOVING EXCEL FOR WINDOWS 95 FEATURES

If there are features that you never use (Microsoft's templates, Data Map, the Analysis ToolPak, and so on), you can remove them to save space. Or if there are features that were not initially installed, you can go back now to add them. Since the process of adding and removing are remarkably similar, we'll cover them both at once. Use the Windows 95 Add/Remove Programs feature to remove unwanted Excel features or add new ones.

1. Choose Settings|Control Panel from the Windows 95 Start menu.

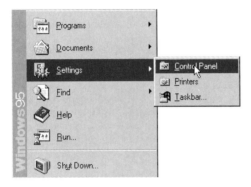

2. Double-click the Add/Remove Programs icon.

3. Click the Install/Uninstall tab if necessary to bring it forward.
4. Click to select either Microsoft Office (if that's how Excel was installed) or Microsoft Excel in the list of programs.

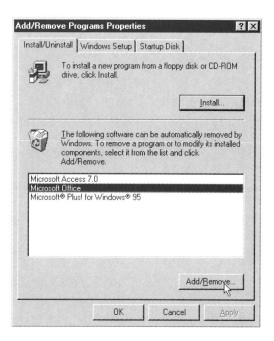

5. Click the Add/Remove button.
6. You will be asked to insert a disk or disc. Click OK when you have complied.
7. You will see a screen advising that the installation has started. Click the Add/Remove button when you see the Installation welcome screen:

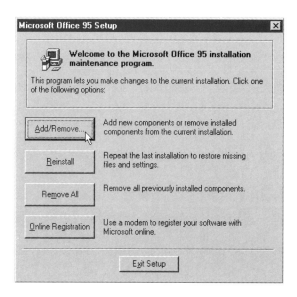

8. If modifying a Microsoft Office installation, choose Excel. If changing a stand-alone Excel installation, skip this step.

9. Click the Change Option button.

10. When presented with the Excel options, pick the category of option you wish to examine. (Add-ins, in this example). Click Change Options again. (Gray boxes indicate that some, but not all of a category's options are installed.)

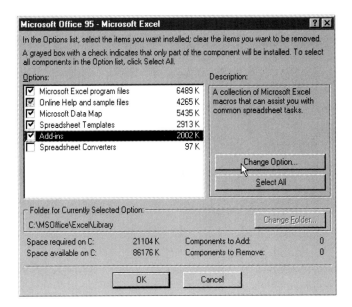

11. You will see a list of items that you can add or remove. Click on an item to read a brief description and see how much disk space it consumes. To add an item on your hard disk, click to place a check mark in the box next to its name. Click to remove check marks for unwanted features. Click OK when done with a particular category, then repeat steps 10 and 11 until all your changes have been specified. When you're back at the option list screen, click OK.

12. Click Continue if you've specified changes, or Cancel if you haven't.

13. The Setup program will make changes if you've specified them or you can click the Exit Setup button to quit without making changes, confirming your choices when asked to do so.

# UNINSTALLING EXCEL

If you hate Excel for Windows 95 for some unimaginable reason, it can be removed by performing steps 1 through 7 above. Click Excel and remove the check mark from its box. The bottom of the screen will indicate that you are removing a large number of files (21 in this example).

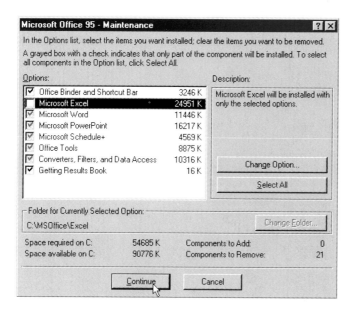

Click Continue if you want to remove Excel, or Cancel if you change your mind. Follow the resulting onscreen prompts.

# APPENDIX B

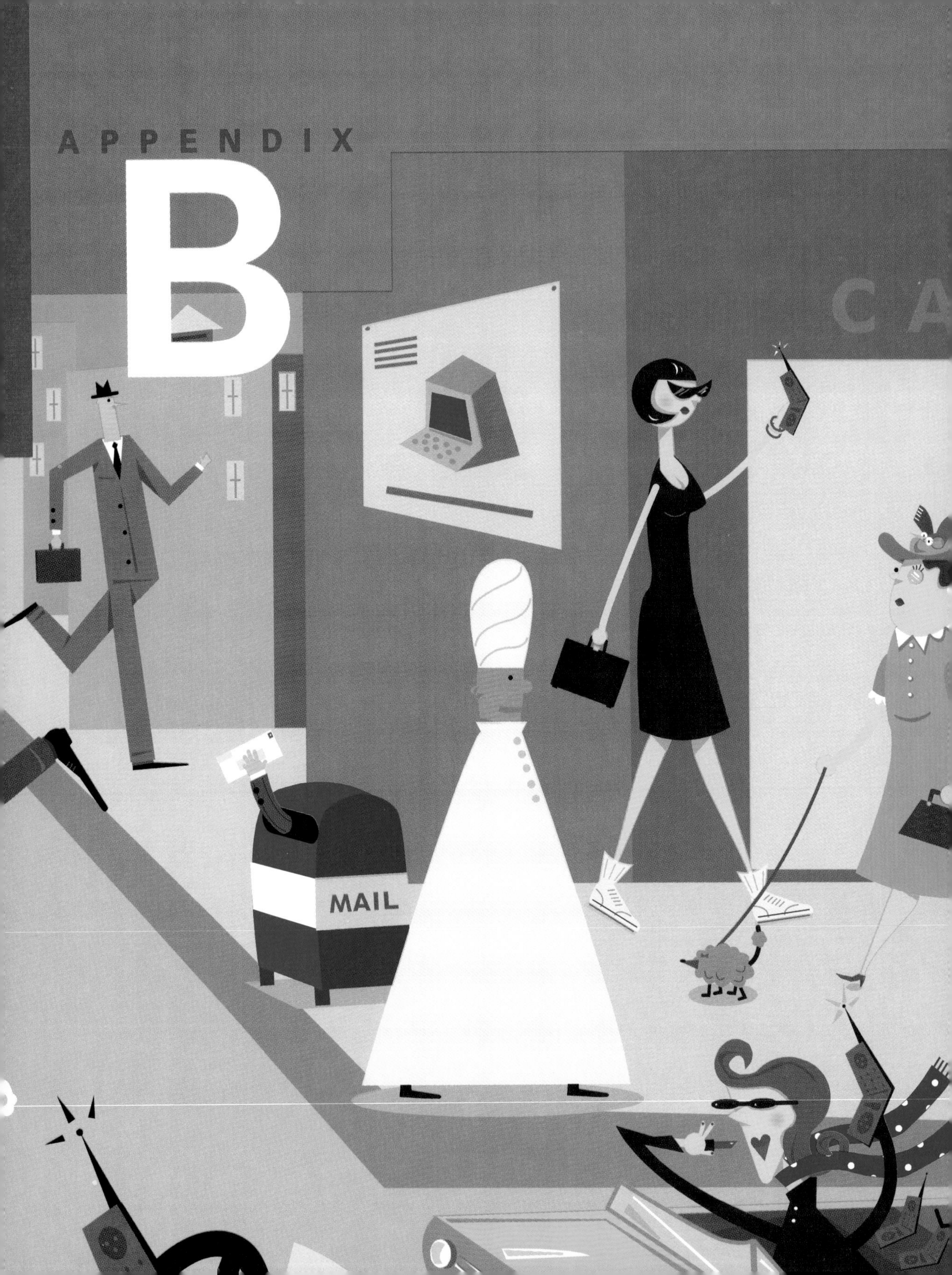

# The Basics of Windows 95

This book assumes that you've already learned the basics of Windows 95, and have perhaps read *Windows 95 for Busy People* (Osborne/McGraw-Hill, 1996). But if you haven't, this appendix should help you get started.

All of Microsoft's Office 95 programs (Word, Excel, PowerPoint, Schedule +, and Access) were especially designed to take advantage of the new Windows 95 operating system. If you know your way around Windows 95, you have a leg up on getting the most out of these and many other programs.

# THE DESKTOP

Windows 95 starts when you turn on your computer. You don't need to type anything first, but you might be asked for a password once or twice. If you don't know one of the passwords, try pressing the ESC key (you should be able to use Windows but you might not have access to your network or to e-mail; so if passwords are required, you should contact your network administrator to set one up). After Windows 95 starts, it displays a screen called the *desktop*. Figure B.1 shows a typical Windows 95 desktop. Yours might look different. That's perfectly OK.

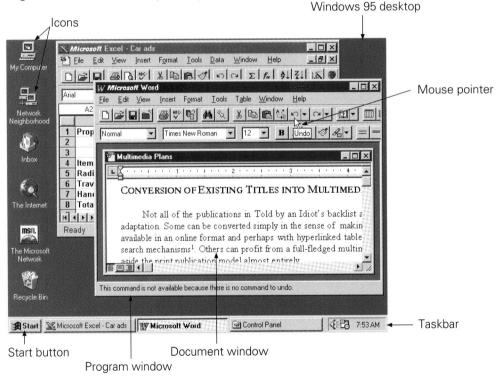

**Figure B.1** A typical Windows 95 desktop

The desktop contains small pictures of items like disk drives, a recycle bin, and so on. These little pictures are called *icons*. At the bottom of the Windows 95 desktop you'll probably see the Taskbar, which will be discussed later in this appendix. Windows 95 also displays *windows*. These windows are the spaces in which you do your work. *Program windows* contain programs (like Word, or Excel, or whatever) and can also contain other windows, often called *document windows* or *child windows*. So, for example, you might have a Word window on your desktop with one or more word processing document windows inside it. Any time you double-click a folder icon (or an icon representing a disk drive), it will open up a window on the screen (and a button on the Taskbar), showing the contents of the folder (or drive).

# MOUSE BASICS

You use the mouse to point to objects on the desktop. (Incidentally, some computers have trackballs or other pointing devices, but all of these devices share some common characteristics: each has at least two buttons, and each lets you point to things.) As you move the mouse or other pointing device, a corresponding *pointer* moves on the desktop. Sometimes the shape of the pointer changes to give you a clue about what you can do next, because what you can do depends on what you're pointing to.

You can also make choices with the mouse (such as choosing a menu option), and you can use it to move and resize objects. You do this by pointing to something and clicking, which usually selects the object or causes something to happen. *Clicking* is accomplished by pressing and releasing a mouse button. *Double-clicking* is the act of pressing and releasing a mouse button twice in rapid succession. *Dragging* is the act of clicking on an object (a window, an icon, or whatever) and moving your mouse while holding down the button.

Most computer pointing devices (mice, trackballs, and so on) have two buttons. If the buttons are side by side, and if you have not modified Windows 95's default mouse settings, you will use the left button for clicking to select things and initiate most actions. You will also use the left button to drag objects around on the desktop and to change the size and shape of things. (Lefties and others who like to customize their environments can switch the functions of the right and left mouse buttons.)

Windows 95 makes extensive use of the right button as well. Clicking the right button (also called *right-clicking*) on almost any screen element will pop up a *shortcut menu* full of useful options. For example, you can change the appearance of your desktop by right-clicking just about anywhere on the desktop and choosing Properties from the menu that pops up. Many programs, including Excel, will display shortcut menus when you use the right mouse button. Examples of right-clicking appear throughout this book.

There is one more mouse technique worth mentioning. It is called *hovering*. Frequently, if you slide the mouse pointer over an object and leave it there for a second, a little message called a *tool tip* will pop up that will tell you something about the object. In Figure B.1, for example, Word is telling you that the button under the mouse pointer is for activating the Undo feature.

# THE TASKBAR

The Taskbar lets you easily run programs and switch from window to window. (If you don't see the Taskbar at the bottom of the desktop, slide your mouse pointer down to the bottom of the screen. The Taskbar should appear.) On the left end of the Taskbar you will always see the Start button. If you have opened windows or started programs (or if Windows has started them for you), your Taskbar will also contain other buttons. See "Taskbar Tips," later, for an explanation of how these buttons work.

# The Start Menu

Let's begin with a look at the Start button and the Start menu that is displayed when you click on it. This is the menu from which you start programs, change Windows settings, retrieve recently used documents, find "lost" files, and get Windows 95 help. You point to items in the Start menu to choose them.

Everyone's Start menu looks a little different, particularly when you scratch the surface. (You can also add shortcuts to programs to the Start menu, such as the Winword item at the top of my menu, shown here.) The Start menu often reveals additional levels of menus called *submenus*. Let's look at the primary Start menu choices.

### Programs

Roughly equivalent to the old Program Manager program groups in earlier versions of Windows, the Programs item on the Start menu pops up a submenu of programs and special Start menu folders. The folders themselves open sub-submenus, and so on. You can run any properly installed program in Windows 95 by clicking on the Start button, then clicking on the Programs choice in the Start menu, and then clicking on the desired program (or perhaps on a folder and then on a program in the folder).

### Documents

The Start menu remembers the last 15 documents you've opened and displays their names in the Documents menu. (However, be forewarned that programs designed prior to Windows 95 often fail to add documents to the Documents menu.) When you want to work with a recently used document again, click on its name in the Documents menu. The document will appear on your screen in the program in which it was created. If the program is not already running, Windows 95 will launch it for you automatically.

### Settings

To change the various settings for your computer, such as the way the Start menu looks or how your screen saver works, choose Settings from the Start menu and then choose Control Panel from the Settings submenu. From the resulting Control Panel window, a part of which is shown here, you can exercise centralized control over all of your computer's settings.

You'll need to consult online help and perhaps read a book like *Windows 95 for Busy People* to learn more about the thousands of possible setting changes.

# Find

Windows 95's Find feature can be an invaluable aid for digging up files that seem to be misplaced. To search for a file, choose Find from the Start menu and then choose Files or Folders. In the dialog box that appears, type a filename or part of one in the Named box and press ENTER or click on Find Now.

# Help

Stuck? Not sure what to do? You can always consult Windows Help. To do so, choose Help from the Start menu. (If you're doing this for the first time, Windows will tell you that it's setting up Help.) In the Help Topics dialog box that appears (see Figure B.2), click on a topic from the expandable Contents list or click on the Index tab, type a key word in the first box, and choose a topic from the index list in the second box.

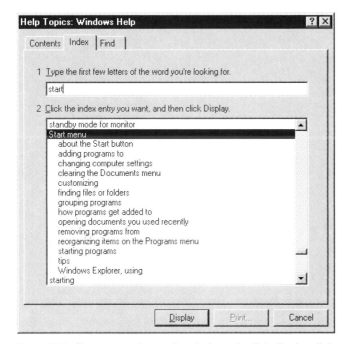

**Figure B.2** Choose a topic or subtopic from the Help Topics dialog box

In most programs, if you're not sure what a button or other screen element does, you can hover the mouse pointer over it for a moment and a tool tip will appear, naming or explaining the object.

Also, in a dialog box, you can click on the What's This? button (a question mark) in the top-right corner and then click on the item in the dialog box that you want more information on. A brief explanation should pop up.

## Run

Any time you know the name of a program file (although sometimes you also have to know the "path" of the folders on the hard disk that leads to the program), you can choose Run from the Start menu, type the name (or path and name) in the box, and press ENTER to run the program. It's usually easier, though, to start the program from the Start menu or one of its submenus.

## Shut Down

When you want to turn off your computer, first shut down Windows 95. To do so, choose Shut Down from the Start menu. Click on Yes when asked if you want to shut down the computer. Wait until Windows tells you it's OK to turn off the computer.

# Taskbar Tips

Every time you start a program or open or minimize some types of windows, the program or window gets its own button on the Taskbar.

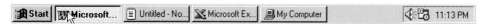

This makes it easy to switch to a program that is already running, to make a particular window active, or to maximize a window. All you have to do is click on the appropriate button on the Taskbar. When a button looks depressed (pushed in), it means that the task represented by the button is the active one, and its window will appear "in front of" the other windows.

If the Taskbar gets too crowded, you can point to its top edge and drag it so that it gets taller. You can also move the Taskbar to any side of the screen (top, bottom, left, or right) by clicking on any part of the Taskbar that is not a button and dragging. When the Taskbar is on the left or right side, you can drag its inner edge to set it to any width, up to half the width of the screen.

# THE MY COMPUTER ICON

One way to explore the files and programs on your computer is to double-click on the My Computer icon. In general, double-clicking on an icon opens it, runs the program it represents, or runs the program in which the document it represents was created. If the icon is a folder or a special icon such as My Computer, it will open into a window and display its contents, which will also appear as icons. Some of these icons might represent programs, and others might represent folders or other special icons.

The My Computer window contains icons that represent your hard disk drive, floppy disk drives, and CD-ROM drive (if applicable), as well as icons for your printers, the Control Panel, and perhaps for dial-up networking.

Double-click on the hard disk drive icon to see the contents of the hard disk. The icon opens into a window that shows folders and other icons. Double-click on any folder to see its contents. Repeat as often as necessary. You can go back up a folder level by pressing BACKSPACE.

# THE NETWORK NEIGHBORHOOD ICON

If your computer is connected to a network, you will see a Network Neighborhood icon on the desktop. Double-clicking on it will show you a list of the remote computers, disk drives, and folders that you can access.

Network Neighborhood

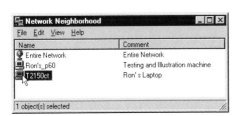

You might need to know the appropriate passwords to access some of the information on the network, and you might be limited in what you can do with files and folders on the network. For example, the owners of some files might let you read the files but not change them. When you have questions, contact your network administrator or help desk.

# THE RECYCLE BIN

When you delete files from your hard disk in Windows 95, they are not immediately erased. They are moved to the Recycle Bin. To recover an accidentally deleted file, double-click on the Recycle Bin icon and choose the item or items you wish to restore. Then choose Restore from the File menu in the Recycle Bin window (see Figure B.3).

Recycle Bin

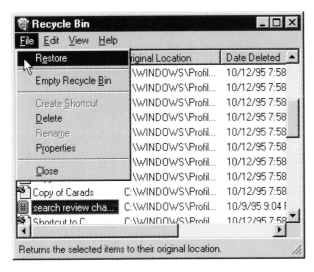

**Figure B.3** The Recycle Bin gives you one more chance to "undelete" your files after trashing them

As you add new files to the Recycle Bin, Windows will eventually start discarding the earliest deleted files left. If you want to free up space, right-click on the Recycle Bin and choose Empty Recycle Bin on the File menu.

# FOLDERS

You and Windows 95 can organize your files into *folders,* which are the equivalent of directories in oldspeak. You can place folders within folders, thereby creating what used to be called subdirectories. You can create a new folder at any point by right-clicking on the desktop or in a folder (or disk drive) window and choosing New | Folder. You can put a document or program in a folder by dragging its icon onto a folder icon or into an open folder window.

# NEW RULES FOR FILENAMES

Windows 95 allows you to use long filenames (up to 255 characters) that include spaces, if you want, so you can give your documents natural sounding names, instead of the pinched, cryptic filenames that DOS used to force on you. Now you can call that document Amortization Projections for 1997 instead of AMTPRJ97.

You might also notice that filename extensions seem to have pretty much disappeared. They're still there at the ends of filenames, but Windows hides all the extensions it recognizes. If you want to see the extensions associated with all filenames, choose Options from the View menu in the My Computer window, the Windows Explorer window, or any folder (or disk drive) window. Click on the View tab. Then uncheck Hide MS-DOS file extensions for file types that are registered. Click on OK. All extensions will appear. To hide most extensions again, repeat the same steps and check the box.

When you are sharing files with non-Windows 95 users, and with programs that were sold prior to the release of Windows 95, filenames get shortened automatically. This can cause some confusion. Again, consult online help and Windows 95 books for details.

# WINDOWS EXPLORER

Windows 95 allows you to look through the folders on your computer in a single window, with the entire folder tree in a pane on the left side (sort of like the old File Manager). To do this, choose Programs from the Start menu and Windows Explorer from the Programs menu (or right-click on any folder and choose Explore from the menu that pops up). The Windows Explorer window will appear (see Figure B.4), with its folder tree in the left pane and the contents of the selected folder in the right pane.

To see the contents of a folder, click on it in the left pane. To expand or collapse a folder's contents, double-click on the folder in the left pane (or click the little plus or minus icon in a box to the left of the folder). You can go up a folder level by pressing BACKSPACE, as you can in any such window.

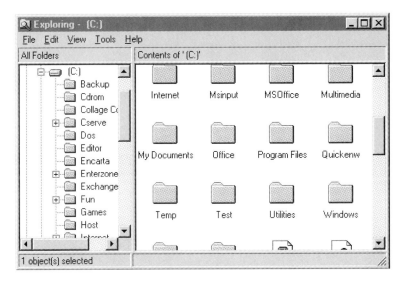

**Figure B.4** The Explorer window shows a hierarchical view of the computer in its left pane. There you can thumb through your tree of folders without having to plow through separate folder windows

# SHORTCUT ICONS

Windows 95 allows you to create *shortcut icons* that "point to" a program, document, folder, or other Windows 95 resource that you use regularly. This is particularly useful when something you use every day is "buried" in a folder within a folder. A popular place to keep shortcuts is on the desktop. That way, when you want to open your favorite folder, you just double-click on the shortcut icon on the desktop. Another place you can create a shortcut is on the Start menu, where it will look like a normal menu choice, not like a shortcut icon.

In general, the easiest way to create a shortcut is to right-click and drag a copy of the program's icon to the place where you want the shortcut. To do this, open the window that contains the program's original icon. Right-click on the icon and drag to a new location, such as another folder or the desktop. When you release the mouse button, a menu will pop up. Choose Create Shortcut(s) Here to make the shortcut. You'll probably want to rename the new shortcut icon. (Press F2, type a new name, and press ENTER.) If you drag an icon onto the Start button, even without first *right*-clicking, a shortcut to that icon will be placed on the Start menu.

# THAT'S THE SHORT COURSE

Well, there you have a taste of Windows 95. Obviously, there's a lot more worth knowing. And the more you learn, the more productive you will become, so I encourage you to do some independent study, either by using Windows 95's online help or by cracking a good book or two.

# Index

**E**